CW01456373

To: _____

From: _____

Date: _____

THE COMPLETE ILLUSTRATED CHILDREN'S BIBLE

DEVOTIONAL

Unless otherwise indicated, all Scripture quotations are taken from the Holy Bible, New International Version®, NIV®. Copyright © 1973, 1978, 1984, 2011 by Biblica, Inc.® Used by permission. All rights reserved worldwide.

Verses marked MSG are taken from THE MESSAGE, copyright © 1993, 1994, 1995, 1996, 2000, 2001, 2002 by Eugene H. Peterson. Used by permission of NavPress. All rights reserved. Represented by Tyndale House Publishers, Inc.

Cover design by Kyler Dougherty

The Complete Illustrated Children's Bible Devotional

Copyright ©2018 North Parade Publishing and International Publishing Services Pty Ltd.

Text from *The Complete Illustrated Children's Bible* by Janice Emmerson
Devotional text commissioned by International Publishing Services
Illustrations by Netscribes

All rights reserved. No part of this publication may be reproduced, stored in a retrieval system, or transmitted in any form or by any means—electronic, mechanical, digital, photocopy, recording, or any other—except for brief quotations in printed reviews, without the prior permission of the publisher.

Printed in China

Contents

The New Testament

THE OLD TESTAMENT

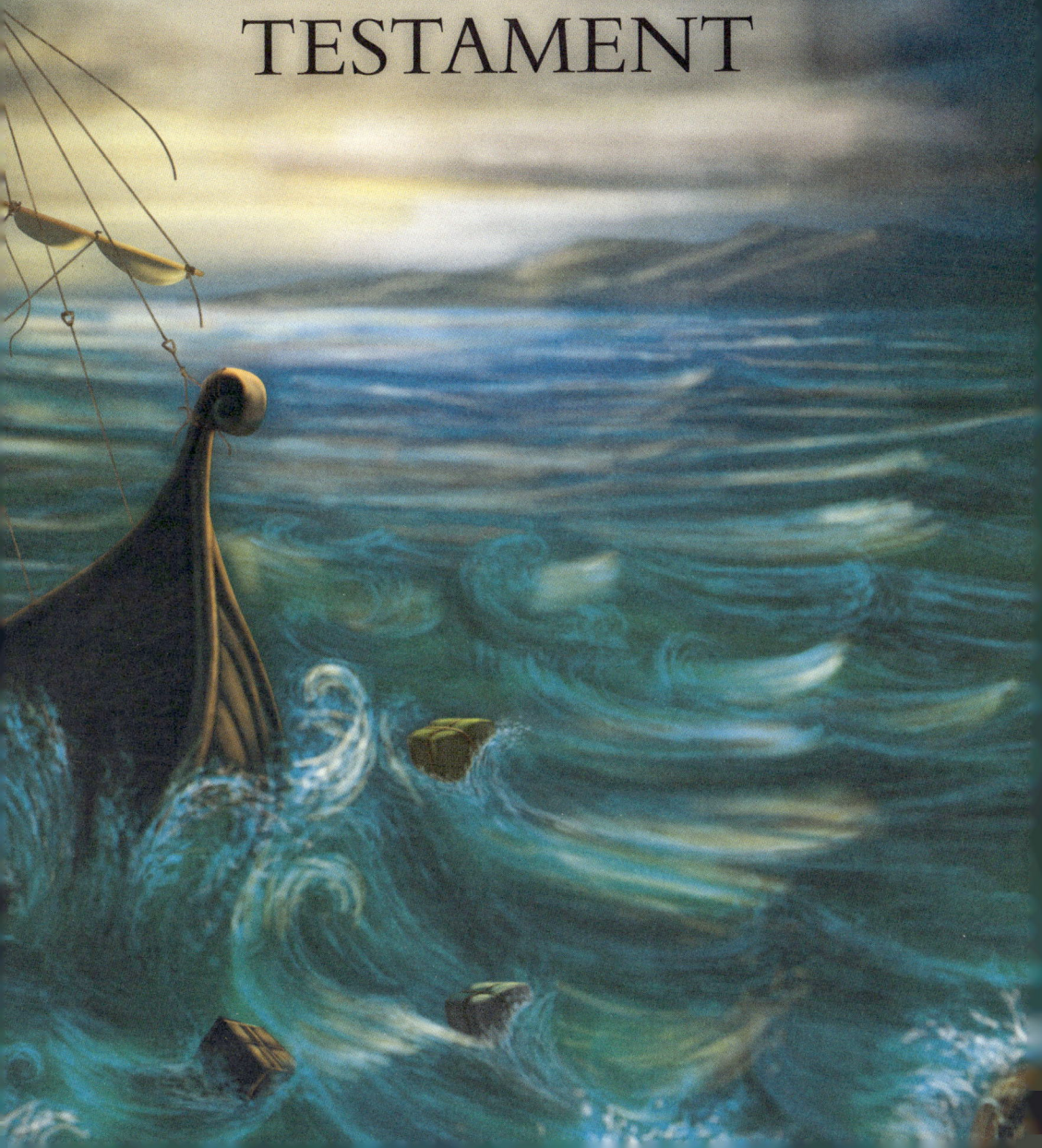

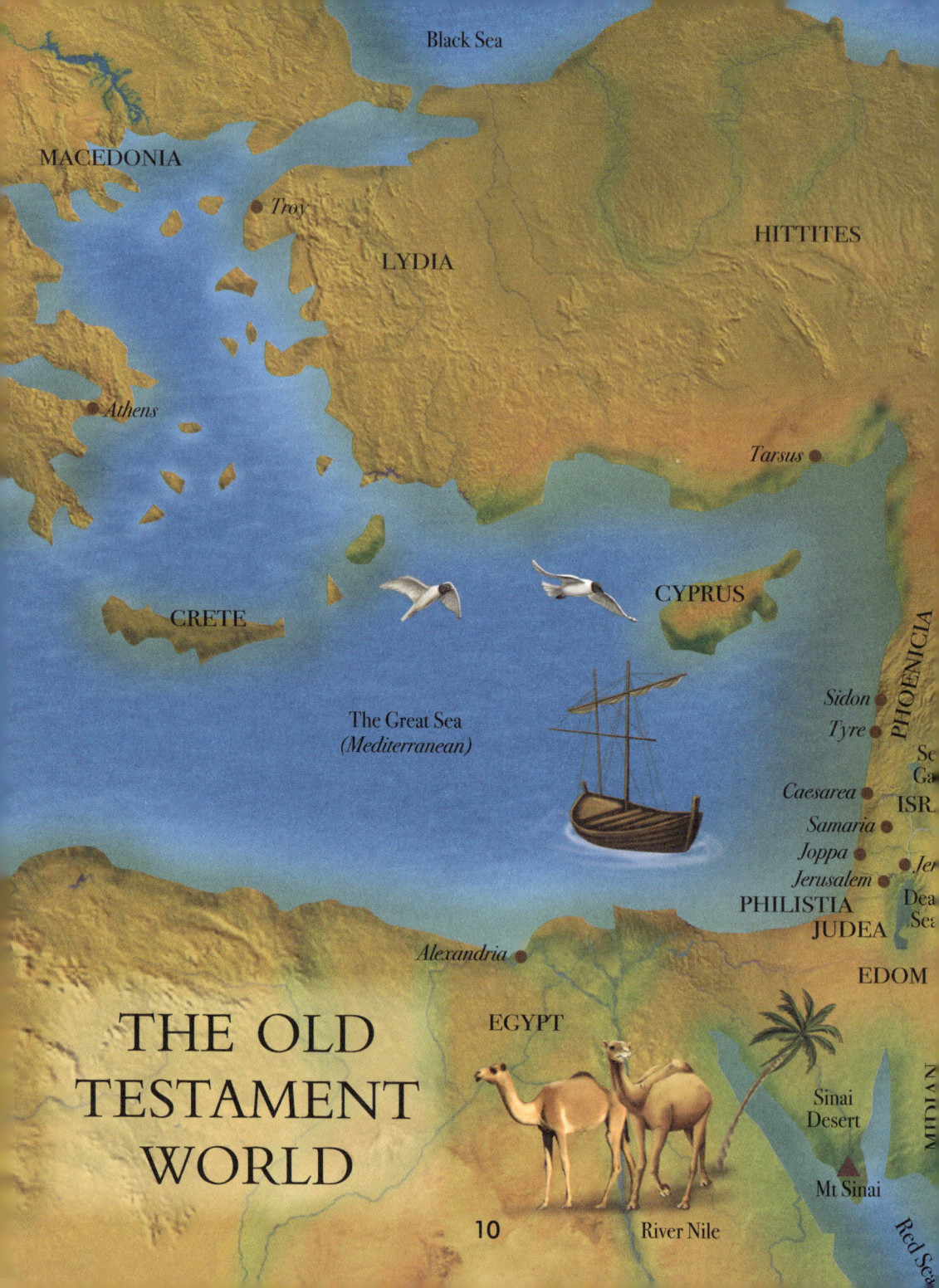

Black Sea

MACEDONIA

Troy

LYDIA

HITTITES

Athens

Tarsus

CRETE

CYPRUS

PHOENICIA

Sidon

Tyre

The Great Sea
(Mediterranean)

Caesarea

Samaria

Joppa

Jerusalem

PHILISTIA

JUDEA

Dea
Sea

Alexandria

EDOM

THE OLD TESTAMENT WORLD

EGYPT

MIDIAN

Sinai
Desert

Mt Sinai

River Nile

Red Sea

ISR

Se
Ga

Jer

Mt Ararat

Caspian Sea

ASSYRIA

Nineveh

River Euphrates

River Tigris

MESOPOTAMIA

MEDIA

RAM

ascus

Babylon

MON

Nippur

Ur

PERSIA

BABYLONIA

Lower Sea
(Persian Gulf)

ARABIA

Arabian Desert

11

GOD MAKES THE WORLD

Genesis 1–2

In the beginning, there was nothing at all. Then God created the heavens and the earth, but everything was still covered in darkness, so God said, "Let there be light," and there was light! God called the light day and the darkness night, and that was the first day and the first night!

In the days that followed, God separated the water from dry land and covered the land with beautiful plants and trees. He made the sun to shine during the day and the moon and stars to light up the night sky.

Then God filled the seas with enormous whales and shiny fish, leaping dolphins and wobbly jellyfish, and he filled the skies with colourful birds. He made animals of all shapes and sizes—swift cheetahs, slow tortoises, huge elephants, and many more.

Last of all, God made man and told him to take care of this wonderful world and all the creatures.

God was pleased with all he had made and done, so on the seventh day he rested and made that day a special day to rest and give thanks.

God Makes the World

Have you ever played with a new puppy? Have you ever snuggled its soft fur and been licked by its little pink tongue? Did you know God invented puppies? Warm fur, waggly tails, and puppy breath are all his ideas.

God is the Great Inventor. When he made the world, he had a blank canvas. He could have made anything he wanted—absolutely anything! And the things that spilled out of his heart and mind—such as watercolour-painted sunsets, birds that serenade us every day, and roly-poly puppies—are very, very good. That's because all God made teaches us one big, beautiful truth about who God is: He is very good.

And guess what? You are God's invention too! Of all of the options God had—tall or short, freckles or no freckles, talkative or shy—he made you! He thought you up, and then he invented you. You are God's very own invention, a God original. And he loves you very much.

> **Dear God,** help me see your good heart in the things you invented. Thank you for this great, good world! **Amen.**

Reflection Questions

1. If you invented something, how would you feel about your invention? Since you are God's invention, what are some things about you that might make God proud?

2. God invented you because he wants to be your very best friend. What are some things you'd like to tell him as your very best friend?

Action Points

1. Take a walk outside today. How can you see God's goodness in nature?

2. Write this on a sticky note and put it on your mirror: "I am God's invention, and he is proud of me!"

DISOBEYING GOD

Genesis 3

Now of all the animals, the most cunning was the snake. One day he said to Eve, "Why don't you eat from the tree of knowledge? The fruit is delicious and it won't harm you! God doesn't want you to eat it because it will make you wise like him. Take a bite!"

The fruit looked so delicious that Eve did pick some and she offered some to Adam too, and they both ate it. At once they realised they were naked and tried to cover themselves with leaves.

When God found Adam and Eve hiding behind some bushes, he knew what had happened and was very angry. He cursed the snake and banished Adam and Eve from the Garden of Eden, telling them that from now on they would have to work hard to make their own food and clothes. Then he placed an angel with a flaming sword to stand guard at the entrance to the garden.

Disobeying God

When God made the world, it shouted one big, beautiful message: "God is good!" But soon after, the snake hissed a dreadful accusation: "No, he's not. He's trying to keep you from something good." It was an awful lie, but Adam and Eve fell for it. They chose not to trust God, and they disobeyed his one rule.

It broke their friendship with God. Adam and Eve now had sin-stained hearts and could not come close to him anymore. And everyone who was born after Adam and Eve would have sin-stained hearts too.

God was so hurt! But he wouldn't give up. He promised he would make a way for his friends to come close to him again. After all, that was the very reason why he had made them. And it is the very same reason he made you too!

When something inside of you hints that you shouldn't obey God, don't listen to it. Instead, come close to him. He made you to be his good friend forever.

Dear God, help me to trust your good heart. Always. **Amen.**

Reflection Questions

1. Has anyone ever betrayed you? How did it make you feel? On a separate sheet of paper, write down some of the feelings you felt.

2. Adam and Eve betrayed God by disobeying him. Even though he was very hurt, he promised to fix what they had broken. What does that tell you about how God felt about them? Since that is how God treats his friends, how do you think he feels when you disobey him? Write down what you think.

Action Points

1. Using a marker, draw an outline of a heart on a piece of white paper. Then colour in the heart with a different colour. Now do your best to get the heart white again. You can't, can you? That's what happened to us—we had sin-stained hearts we couldn't get clean. But God promised he would not leave us that way.

2. God gave Adam and Eve one rule because he wanted to protect them. When your parents give you rules, they are trying to protect you too. Obeying their rules is one way you can show them you love them. Do your best today to show you love your parents by obeying the rules they've set for you.

THE FLOOD
Genesis 6–9

God warned Noah that a huge flood was coming. He told Noah to build an enormous boat, an ark, so that he and his family might be saved along with two of every living creature. When the ark was finished, Noah loaded it with food for his family and the animals, and then God sent the animals to the ark, two by two, one male and one female of every kind.

When they were all safely in, it began to rain. Water poured down from the skies and covered all the land. Every living creature was drowned. All the towns and cities were washed away. But the ark and its precious cargo floated free on a world of water.

For 40 days and 40 nights it rained. Then, at last, it stopped. After a while, the floodwaters began to go down. Noah sent out a dove and, when it returned with an olive leaf in its beak, Noah knew that the flood was over, for the trees were growing again.

Then it was time for Noah and the animals to leave the ark. Noah was filled with gratitude, and God promised that he would never again send such a dreadful flood. He put a beautiful rainbow in the sky to remind Noah of this promise.

The Flood

Have you ever seen a rainbow? Noah saw the very first one.

Life on earth had got so bad that the only thoughts that people had were evil. So God sent a flood and started the world over with his only friend, Noah.

God made his friend a promise: "I will never destroy the earth again with a flood." Then he put a rainbow in the sky as a forever reminder of his promise.

Have you ever seen a bow, like from a bow and arrow? To shoot an arrow, you pull the string, and the bow bends—just like the shape of a rainbow.

You see, even though God had given people a do-over to follow him, he knew their hearts still were not clean. He knew people would still sin. And he knew someone would need to be punished. But God wasn't going to punish people with a flood again. The bow of a rainbow points the arrow towards heaven. God was saying, "This time I'll take the punishment myself." And with Jesus, he did.

Dear God, when I see a rainbow, help me remember you sent Jesus to take the punishment for my sins so I could be your friend forever. Thank you so much! **Amen.**

Reflection Questions

1. Using a pencil, make a list of some things you have done wrong. When Jesus died for you, he not only paid for your sins but also gave you a clean heart. It was a complete do-over. Now, using an eraser, do your best to completely erase your list.

2. Jesus gave his life to take the punishment for the things you have done wrong, so how must he feel about you? On top of where your list of wrongs used to be, write how God feels about you.

Action Points

1. On a piece of white paper, draw and colour a rainbow. As you do, thank God for sending Jesus.

2. Do you know someone who needs to know what Jesus has done for them? Talk to God and ask him to help you share Jesus's story with them.

GOD'S PROMISE
Genesis 15–17

Abraham was a good man who trusted God. He and his wife, Sarah, were very old and hadn't had a child. But one day, God told him that he would be a father. In fact, he would have too many descendants to count, and the land would belong to them. Then God told him to prepare a sacrifice.

That evening God spoke to him again, telling him that his descendants would be slaves in a country not their own for 400 years. But they would at last be free and would return to their own land, and those who had enslaved them would be punished.

When the sun had set and darkness had fallen, a smoking firepot with a blazing torch appeared and passed between the pieces of the sacrifice as a sign to Abraham from God.

God's Promise

Have you ever made a promise? God made a big promise to his friend Abraham.

To show how serious he was about his promise, God did something that seems odd to us today. He asked Abraham to kill some animals and arrange the pieces in two lines. It was one of the ways people made agreements back then, like a handshake today. The people making the deal would walk between the animal pieces. It was their way of saying, "If I don't keep my word, you can walk around in my blood, just as we are walking around in the blood of these animals."

But Abraham never really walked between the animal pieces. Only God did—he walked through in a fiery form. God was going to keep both sides of the promise. He was saying, "Even if you don't keep your end of this bargain, you can walk around in *my* blood." God was going to bless Abraham, and Abraham didn't need to do anything to make it happen.

And one of Abraham's distant relatives would be a blessing to the whole world—Jesus would rescue us all!

Dear God, thank you for doing everything to rescue us. I love you! **Amen.**

Reflection Questions

1. God was so determined to rescue everyone that he took care of everything himself. How does that make you feel? Write down some words that describe your feelings.

2. God went to great lengths to rescue the people he created—including you! List some words to describe how God must feel about you.

Action Points

1. Make up a song of thanks to God for saving you and sing it to him. Don't worry about making up perfect lyrics—just sing the words as they come to your heart!

2. What are some things you can do today to keep your word, as God did with his promise? Maybe it is doing your homework, or maybe it is cleaning your room as you told your mum you would. Now, go and do them!

ISAAC IS BORN

Genesis 21

When Sarah was 90 years old, she gave birth to a baby boy, Isaac, just as God had promised. Abraham and Sarah were overjoyed, but Sarah believed her maidservant Hagar was making fun of her. She was so angry with her that she made Abraham send Hagar away, along with her son, Ishmael, who was also Abraham's son.

Abraham was sad, but God told him things would work out for Ishmael, so he handed Hagar some food and water and sent her and Ishmael into the desert.

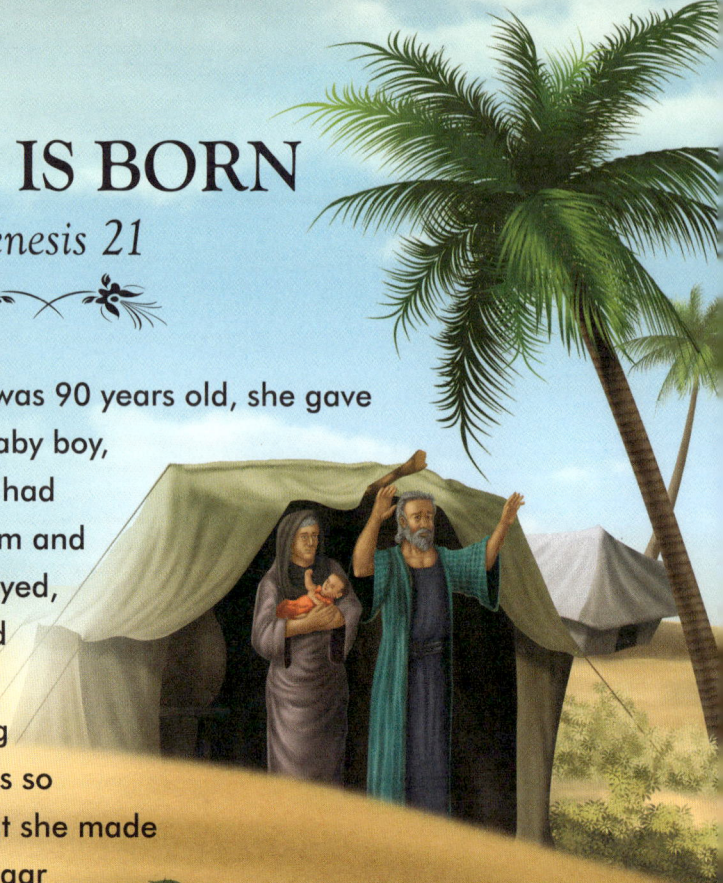

Soon all the water was gone, and they began to weep. But the angel of God called to Hagar from heaven and said, "Do not be afraid, Hagar. God has heard the boy crying. Lift him up and take him by the hand, for he will be the father of a great nation." Then God opened her eyes, and she saw a well of water!

God was with the boy as he grew up. He lived in the desert and became an archer.

Isaac Is Born

Sarah laughed when she overheard God telling Abraham she was going to have a baby. She was 89 years old, and Abraham was 99! And when she had a baby boy at 90 years old, she must have laughed again, because that is what she named him—Isaac, which means "laughter."

It is such a fun adventure to be God's kid. Just as he was with Abraham and with Sarah, God is on this adventure of life with you. He lives inside of you through his Holy Spirit. And he wants you to learn something from Sarah and Abraham's story: Nothing is impossible for him.

That means the God for whom nothing is impossible is walking through life with you. Right now. In every situation you face, God is living inside of you. Your maths test. Football practice. Your ballet recital. And when you ask him for help, it is fun to see how he—the God who can do anything—answers.

Dear God, help me believe with all my heart that you can do anything and that you live inside of me. That is so much fun! **Amen.**

Reflection Questions

1. Think of something you are facing right now. God can do anything, and he lives inside of you. How does that change the way you face that situation? Write down your thoughts.

2. God is good, and he loves to do good things. So what are some areas of your life where you can let him be more involved? Write down some things, and then ask him for help in those areas.

Action Points

1. Is there someone in your life who needs to know God can do anything? Make a card to encourage them. And as you do, ask God to get involved in their life.

2. Write this saying of Jesus on a piece of paper and try to memorise it today: "I am with you always" (Matthew 28:20).

ABRAHAM IS TESTED
Genesis 22

❧❧❧

I saac grew up to be a fine young boy, and his father and mother were very proud of him and thankful to God. But one day, God decided to test Abraham's faith. He told Abraham that he must offer the boy as a sacrifice!

Abraham was heartbroken, but his faith in God was absolute, and so he prepared everything, just as he had been commanded.

But as he lifted up his knife, suddenly an angel spoke to him. "Abraham, Abraham! Do not harm the boy! I know now that you love the Lord your God with all your heart, for you would be willing to give up your own son."

God sent a ram to be sacrificed in the boy's place, and the angel told Abraham that God would truly bless him and his descendants because of his faith.

Abraham Is Tested

This is a really hard story, isn't it?

It is a hard story from the point of view of both Abraham and Isaac. Even though Isaac was about to be killed, he did not struggle; he trusted his father. And even though God was telling Abraham to kill his precious son, Abraham trusted God. It was a very tense situation.

But every bit of the tension we feel is also there in another Father-Son event that happened thousands of years later when Jesus was on the cross. He could have struggled or got down, but he didn't. He trusted his Father. And God could have stopped the people from killing Jesus, but he didn't. He knew it was the only way to rescue us all.

God stopped Abraham from killing Isaac. But God did not stop Jesus from dying on the cross. The force of the nails—as hard as it is to think about—was the force of God's love. At the cross God shouted, "I love you!"

Dear Jesus, thank you for giving your life to save me. I am so thankful. **Amen.**

Reflection Questions

1. How do you think Abraham felt while he was getting ready to sacrifice Isaac? How do you think Isaac felt when he realised what his father was going to do? Write down your thoughts.

2. It's hard to explain, but God is the Father, the Son, and the Holy Spirit. How does it make you feel that God the Father loves you so much that he was willing to let his one and only Son die for you? And how does it make you feel that God the Son, Jesus, loves you so much that he gave his life for you? Write down your feelings.

Action Points

1. God shouted, "I love you!" from the cross. Is there someone who needs to know how much you love them—a parent or a best friend? Don't wait! Tell them today that you love them very much.

2. Spend some time alone today with God and tell him how much you love him.

JACOB AND ESAU
Genesis 25–27

Isaac grew up and married a beautiful woman named Rebekah. She was old before she became pregnant, and when she did, it was with twins. God told her that the two boys would one day be the fathers of two nations. The firstborn was a hairy boy, whom they named Esau, and his brother was called Jacob. When they grew up, Esau became a great hunter, while Jacob was quieter and spent more time at home. Isaac loved Esau, but Rebekah was especially fond of Jacob.

One day Jacob was preparing a stew when his brother came in ravenous after a long trip. Esau was so hungry that when Jacob told him he could only have a plate of stew in exchange for his birthright, he agreed!

In later years, Jacob cheated his elder brother out of his father's blessing too. When Isaac was very old and nearly blind, he wished to give his blessing to his eldest son, Esau. Jacob, with the help of his mother, disguised himself as Esau. He wore goatskins around his arms so that he would be hairy like his brother. When his father touched him, he believed him to be Esau and gave him his blessing to be in charge of the family when he died.

When Esau found out what had happened, he was so angry that he wanted to kill his younger brother, so Rebekah sent Jacob away from home where he would be safe.

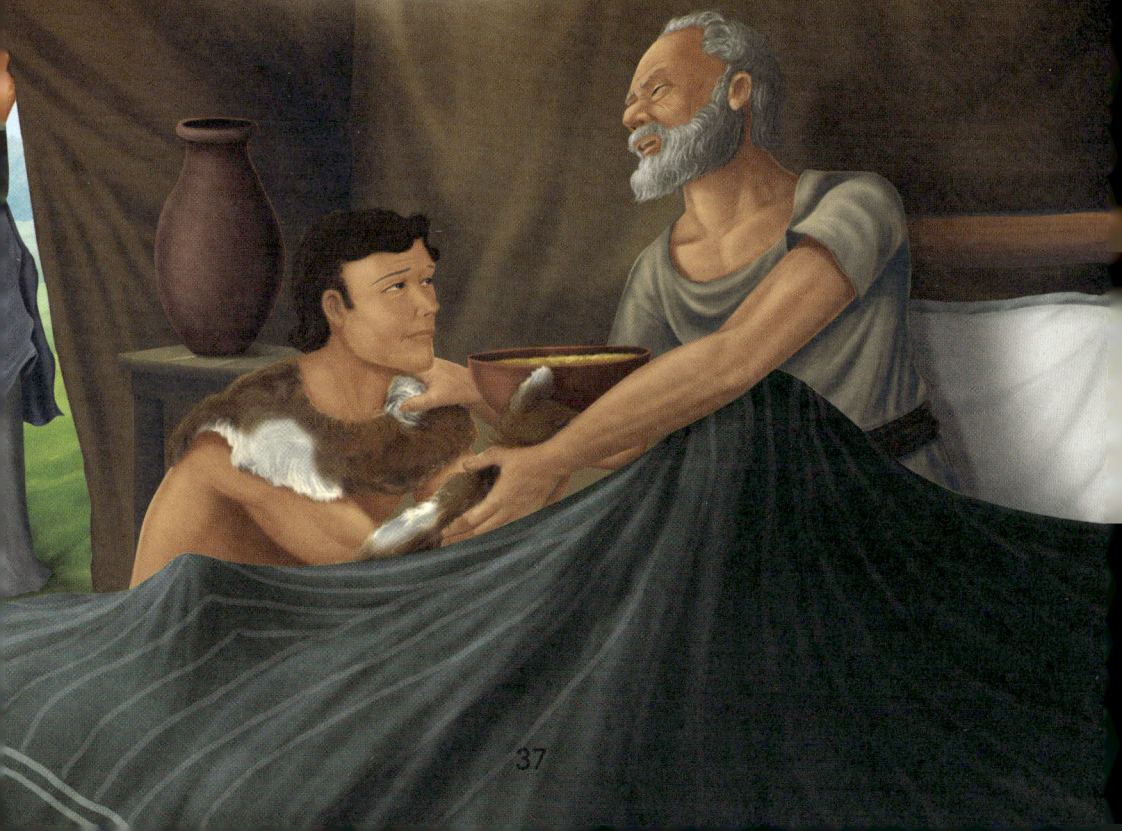

Jacob and Esau

When Isaac's wife, Rebekah, was pregnant with twins, God told her the older boy would serve the younger one (Genesis 25:23). That was not the way things normally went. But God knew that was how it would be. When Isaac accidentally gave the family blessing to Jacob instead of Esau, Isaac was surprised. But God wasn't.

That's because God knows everything. And what's even more awesome is this: Since God is good, he is always working for good. Romans 8:28 says, "In all things God works for the good of those who love him." That means the God who is king over everything is always up to something good in your life. Always. Every single minute.

God can use the hardest thing in your life for good. He can use the saddest thing in your life for good. And he can use anything you go through or any situation you face for good. How wonderful is that?

Dear God, thank you for being good and for always working for good! Please teach me to trust you. **Amen.**

Reflection Questions

1. Are you going through anything hard right now? In a few words, write down what is happening.

2. If you could see what God sees about the situations in your life, you would see how he is working for good. How could God be working for good in the situations you wrote about? Write down some of your thoughts.

Action Points

1. Talk to God about the situations you wrote about, and ask him to help you trust him. And remember that he is working for good even in these hard things.

2. Is someone in your life going through a hard time? Ask God to show you a way you can help them. Maybe your little sister needs help understanding her maths. Maybe the new guy at school needs someone to sit with at lunch. Maybe your coach needs prayer. Once God shows you something you can do, go and do it!

WRESTLING WITH GOD
Genesis 32–33

Jacob lived with his Uncle Laban for many years and got married. When he finally decided to return home with his family, he was worried, for he did not know how his brother, Esau, would greet him. When a messenger said that Esau was coming to meet him with 400 men, Jacob sent some of his servants ahead with gifts for his brother. Then he sent his family and everything he owned across the river. Jacob himself stayed behind alone to pray.

Suddenly a man appeared, and the two of them wrestled together until daybreak. When the man saw that he could not overpower him, he touched Jacob's hip so that it was wrenched. He asked Jacob to let him go, but Jacob replied, "Not unless you bless me."

Then the man said, "Your name will no longer be Jacob but Israel because you have struggled with God and with men and have overcome."

When Jacob asked his name, he would give no reply, but blessed Jacob. Then Jacob understood that he had wrestled with God himself!

And when Jacob finally came face-to-face with his brother, he found that Esau had forgiven him and welcomed him with open arms.

41

Wrestling with God

To wrestle someone, you have to get really close to them, don't you? You have to get down on their level until you are face-to-face.

That is what God did with Jacob.

God is the king of all. He commands armies of angels. He is in charge of the earth and the whole universe. He is really big—in fact, he is infinite! But he wanted to be really close to Jacob.

Jacob was worried about seeing his brother the next day. The last he knew, Esau wanted to kill him. So he was probably scared. He needed to know God was close. So God came close because he is a good friend.

That is the kind of friendship God wants to have with you. Even though he is God and is always doing God things, God wants to be super close with you. Even though he is the king of all, he loves you, cares about you, and wants to be your very best friend.

Dear God, thank you for wanting to be my best friend. I would love that! **Amen.**

Reflection Questions

1. Think about your best friend. Why is that person your best friend? Write out some reasons.

2. Best friends spend time together. Best friends tell each other everything. They talk all the time. Since God wants to be your best friend, is there anything you want to tell him? Write it down.

Action Points

1. What is your favourite thing to do when you are by yourself? Invite God to do it with you today. Since he is always with you, just turn your attention to him. Talk to him. Good friendships grow when you do things together and when you share your hearts with each other. Hang out with God today.

2. Friends are important. Pay attention at school the next few days. Is there someone who needs a friend? How could you be kind to that person?

BROTHER FOR SALE
Genesis 37

Jacob lived in Canaan. He had 12 sons, but Joseph was his favourite. Joseph's brothers were terribly jealous of Joseph, and eventually they decided to get rid of him. One day when they were out in the fields, they set upon him, tearing off a beautiful coat his father had given him and throwing him into a deep pit. Then they sat down nearby to eat, deaf to his cries for help.

Shortly, they saw a caravan of Ishmaelite traders passing by on their camels on their way to Egypt. Quick as a flash they decided to sell Joseph to the traders.

Then they took his beautiful coat and smeared it with the blood of a goat. Afterwards, they trooped home with long faces and showed the coat to their father, saying that Joseph had been killed by a wild animal. Jacob was heartbroken at the death of his beloved son.

Brother for Sale

Joseph's brothers lied, cheated, and sold him into slavery. It was awful.

Sometimes life can be really hard. You would think following God would make life easy, wouldn't you? But it doesn't. Even people who do their best go through hard things.

God understands. That is because he has felt a hurting heart.

In heaven, angels surround Jesus and sing his praises. But on Earth he was often surrounded by people who mocked him. While Jesus was on Earth, he was kind and loving to people, but they were often mean to him. Jesus did not do anything wrong, but people said he was a criminal, and they killed him.

God knows about unfair and hard things because he has experienced them himself.

When you go through something difficult, God sees your hurting heart, and he knows how you feel. Tell him how you are feeling, and let him comfort you. And know this: We won't experience pain forever because when Jesus comes back to Earth, he is going to make everything right. Forever. And we will never hurt again.

Dear God, please comfort my heart
when it is hurting. I cannot wait for you to
make everything right again! **Amen.**

Reflection Questions

1. When Jesus's dear friends Mary and Martha were sad because their brother had died, Jesus wept (John 11:35). Can you imagine God crying? How do you think God feels when you are going through something sad? Write down some of the feelings you think he might have.

2. When Jesus comes back to Earth, he is going to fix everything that is broken. What are some things that you cannot wait for him to make right again? Make a list.

Action Points

1. When we are sad, telling other people about what we are going through can cheer up our hearts. If you are feeling sad, share your feelings with your parents or a close friend. Invite them to walk through the hard time with you.

2. Maybe you are not going through a hard time, but you know someone who is. How can you help them during their time of sadness? Go and do it!

THE BROTHERS BUY GRAIN
Genesis 42–43

God blessed Joseph in Egypt and gave him wisdom. He became a great leader—second only to Pharaoh—and saved the land during a terrible famine. Joseph's family was still in Canaan, and the famine hit them hard too. Jacob decided to send his sons to buy grain in Egypt. When they reached Egypt, the brothers bowed down before Joseph. With his golden chain and fine clothes, they did not recognise him, but Joseph recognised them.

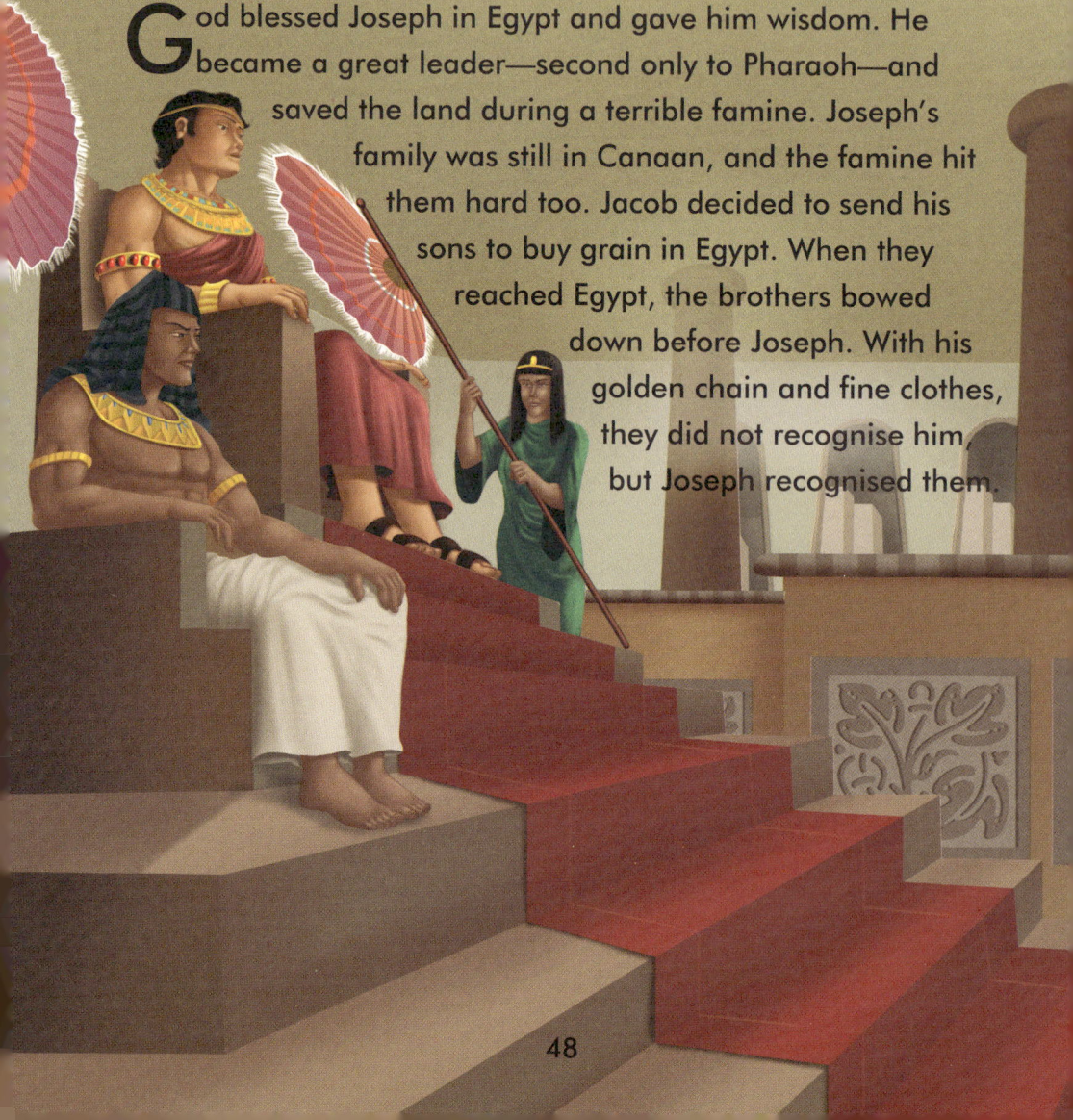

Joseph wanted to see if his brothers had changed at all, so he planned to test their honesty and loyalty. He accused them of being spies, and when they protested their innocence, he agreed to let them go back to Canaan with grain, on the condition that they returned with their youngest brother, Benjamin, whom Joseph had never met.

Jacob did not want to let Benjamin go, but in the end he had to agree. So the brothers returned with more money to pay for the grain.

The Brothers Buy Grain

More than ten years had passed since Joseph's brothers sold him into slavery. Joseph could have held a grudge against his brothers for all those years, but he didn't. Joseph forgave his brothers for all they had done to him.

When someone wrongs you, it is very hard. Many times the person cannot (or will not) fix what they have broken. So you have a choice. You can hold on to bitterness and anger, or you can forgive them and choose not to make them pay for their wrong. If you hold on to the bitterness, you are adding new pain to the pain they caused. But if you forgive them, just as Joseph forgave his brothers, you can be free.

Forgiveness does not mean saying what someone did was okay. If someone hurts you, that is not okay. By choosing forgiveness, you may still be sad about what happened, but you make the choice to let go of the pain. You set them free—and that sets you free as well.

Dear God, please give me the courage to forgive. I want to be free! **Amen.**

Reflection Questions

1. Do you need to forgive someone? The first part of forgiveness is naming what the person took from you when they hurt you. How did their actions affect you? Write down some of the ways.

2. The second part of forgiving is being sad over what you lost. Look at your list. Let yourself be sad about what you lost. But the final part of forgiveness is choosing not to make someone pay for what they did. Write this statement below, and ask God to help you mean it: "God, what this person did to me was wrong. I'm sad about it. But help me forgive them for what they did so I can be free."

Action Points

1. Is there anything for which you need to ask someone's forgiveness? Talk to them, say you are sorry, and ask them to forgive you.

2. If you know Jesus, God has forgiven you for every wrong you have ever committed. Today, thank God for his forgiveness and ask him to help you be a good forgiver—just like him.

THE LONG-LOST BROTHER

Genesis 43–45

Joseph was so overcome when he saw Benjamin that he had to hide his face. He had his servants feed the brothers, then sent them on their way with more food, but not before hiding a silver cup in Benjamin's sack.

The brothers were travelling home when guards came upon them and dragged them back to the palace. "Thieves!" shouted Joseph. "I treated you with kindness, and you repay me by stealing!"

"There must be some mistake!" cried the brothers, but when the guards checked, there was the silver cup in Benjamin's sack. The brothers fell to their knees. "My lord," they cried, "take any one of us, but do not take Benjamin, for his father's heart would break!"

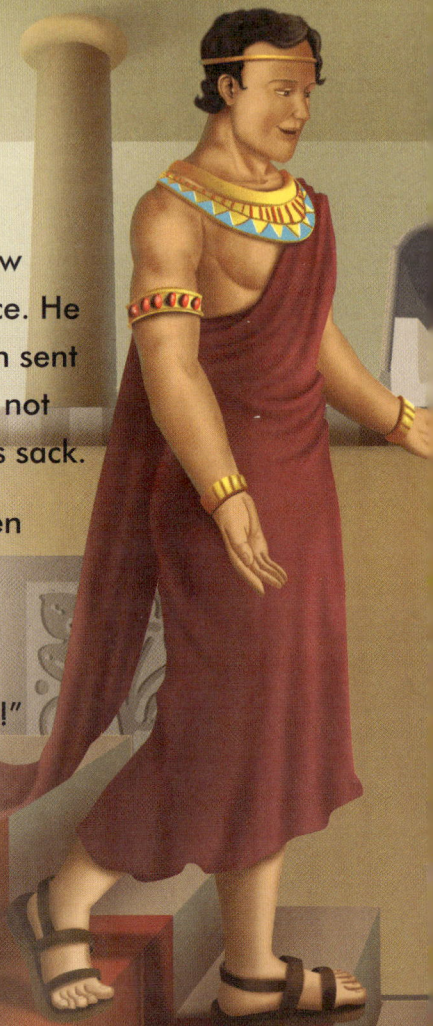

At this, Joseph knew that his brothers' hearts were no longer hard, and so he hugged them. Amid much weeping and amazement, he told them that he was their long-lost brother, and that they should not feel too guilty, for it had all been part of the Lord's plan. "I was sent to rule in Egypt so that you would not starve in Canaan!" he told them, and then he sent for his father.

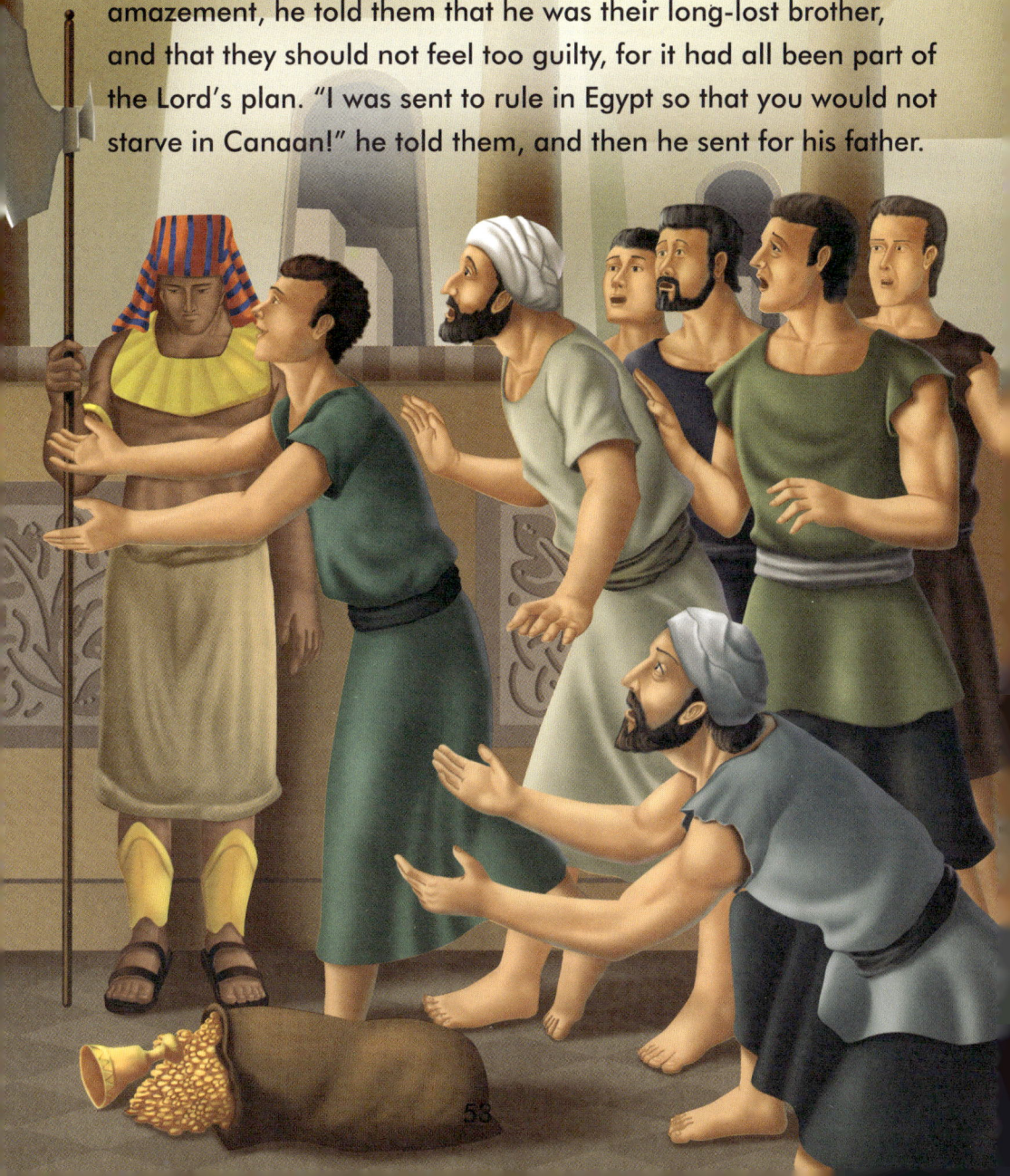

The Long-Lost Brother

Have you ever been laughed at? Or had your feelings hurt? Or got into trouble for something you didn't do? Joseph went through all those things—and worse! Because of his brothers, he was kidnapped, forced to be a slave, and even thrown in jail! But when Joseph had the chance to get even with brothers, he didn't. He forgave them instead. Joseph knew that God had used his brothers' evil plans to do something great and save many lives.

God can use your tough times too. He might use being laughed at to help you be kinder to others, or he might use someone's lies to teach you how important the truth is. When you trust God, he'll help you through your troubles, and he'll use them to do great things.

Dear God, when bad things happen, help me remember that you can use them for great good. **Amen.**

Reflection Questions

1. The truth is that people won't always be kind to you. But it's how you handle those people that matters most. Will you try to get even? Or will you choose to forgive instead?

2. Has anyone ever made fun of you? What are some words that describe how that made you feel? How do you feel when you see someone else being made fun of?

Action Points

1. Is there someone at your school that the other kids make fun of? Think of at least one thing that person is really good at—and then tell them about it.

2. Jesus said, "Love your enemies" (Matthew 5:44). Is someone in your life hard to love or even like? Make it a point to do something kind for that person today.

A BABY IN THE REEDS

Exodus 2

Many years passed, and Egypt's new king turned Jacob's descendants—the Hebrews—into slaves. He even ordered that when Hebrew boys were born, they must be killed.

Moses was a beautiful baby boy. His mother loved him dearly, but she knew that if the king found out about him, he would be killed. So she made a basket, wrapped her baby in a shawl, placed him in it, and lowered him into the Nile River among the reeds.

After a while, the king's daughter came down to the river. She noticed the basket and saw a crying child inside. "This must be one of the Hebrew babies," she said softly.

Moses's sister, Miriam, was secretly watching from nearby. Now she bravely stepped forward and offered to fetch someone to nurse the baby. When the princess nodded, Miriam darted off to find her own mother. So it was that Miriam's mother looked after her own son, until he was old enough for the princess to take him to the palace.

A Baby in the Reeds

Think of all the different people who watch over you and take care of you. Can you even count them all? Family and friends. Teachers, policemen, and firemen. These people help you, protect you, and keep you safe.

Did you know there's someone else who watches over you too? It's God! Just as God protected Moses from the dangerous river and the evil king, he takes care of you. God watches over you day and night. He doesn't even sleep (Psalm 121:3-5)! He never leaves you alone, and he's never too busy to listen whenever you want to talk. So if you're ever feeling frightened or lonely, remember that God is always there, and he's always watching over you. Why? Because he loves you!

> **Dear God,** thank you for always watching over me. I know you love me, so I will trust you to take care of me. **Amen.**

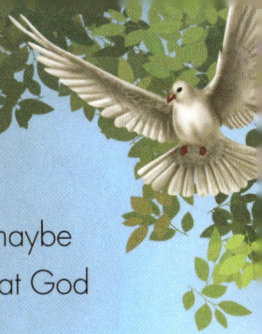

Reflection Questions

1. What frightens you? Is it talking to someone new? Or maybe it's storms or the dark. How does it help you to know that God is always right there beside you?

2. God is so big and powerful, he can watch over every single person, every single second of the day and night. Write a prayer thanking God for watching over you.

Action Points

1. Think of a person who watches out for you and keeps you safe. It might be a parent, a neighbour, or a teacher. How can you say thank you? Plan something special and then do it this week.

2. Some people—like policemen, firemen, and soldiers—watch over your whole neighbourhood. Do something special for one of them. Bake some cookies, make a card, or simply say thank you.

THE BURNING BUSH

Exodus 3–4

When Moses grew up, he was shocked to see how the Egyptians treated his fellow Hebrews. After killing an Egyptian for beating a Hebrew slave, he had to leave Egypt and became a shepherd. One day while Moses was tending his sheep, he noticed that a nearby bush was on fire, yet the leaves of the bush were not burning! As he stepped closer, he heard the voice of God. "Take off your sandals, Moses, for this is holy ground. I am the God of your father, the God of Abraham, of Isaac, and of Jacob." Moses hid his face in fear.

The Lord said, "I have come to rescue my people and bring them up out of Egypt into the Promised Land. You must go to Pharaoh and demand that he free them."

Moses was terrified at the thought of speaking to Pharaoh, but God told him that he would be with him, and that he should tell Pharaoh that it was Yahweh* who sent him. He promised that he would perform many miracles so that in the end Pharaoh would let the Hebrews go.

Moses was scared, but God would not listen to his excuses and sent him back to Egypt, although he did send Moses's brother, Aaron, to help him.

* The Hebrew word *Yahweh* is a sacred name for God among the Jewish people and translates as "I am who I am."

The Burning Bush

Do you ever feel as if God is asking you to do something that's just too hard? Like love your enemy, stand up for what's right, or forgive someone who hurt your feelings? Sometimes God will ask you to do hard things. But he also stays right there with you and gives you everything you need to do what he wants you to do.

Think about Moses. He was terrified of talking to Pharaoh, but that's exactly what God told Moses he must do. Did God send Moses off to do it all by himself? No! God went with him, and he sent Moses's brother, Aaron, to help him. Yes, God will ask you to do some tough things, but he'll always be right there beside you to help.

Dear God, sometimes it's hard to do the things you want me to do. Thank you for always being there to help me. **Amen.**

Reflection Questions

1. Is there something you're struggling to do? Maybe it's forgiving someone or being kind to someone who's not very nice to you. Write it on a piece of paper, and take some time to pray and ask God to help you.

2. God sent Aaron to help Moses. Has God ever sent someone to help you when you needed to do something hard? Write down a few examples.

Action Points

1. You can be the person God sends to help someone do what he wants them to do. Encourage someone to do the right thing today—offer to help, pray with them, or simply stand up beside them.

2. Telling people about God isn't always easy, but it's one of the most important things you'll ever do. Tell someone about God today.

THE PLAGUES

Exodus 7–11

Moses and Aaron asked Pharaoh to let God's people go into the desert to hold a festival, but Pharaoh said no. So the Lord sent a series of plagues upon the Egyptians. He changed the waters of the Nile into blood so that all the fish died and the air stank. He sent frogs that covered the countryside and filled the houses. He turned the dust on the ground into gnats, and after them came a swarm of flies—so many that the air was black with them. He sent a plague among the livestock of the land but spared the animals belonging to the Hebrews. Then the Egyptians were afflicted with horrible boils.

Next God sent a terrible hailstorm, which stripped the land. Then those plants that had managed to survive were consumed by a swarm of locusts. Nothing green remained on tree or plant in all the land of Egypt. After this, God sent total darkness to cover Egypt for three days.

The final plague was the worst. Moses warned Pharaoh that at midnight, every firstborn son in the land would die, but the sons of the Israelites would be spared. Still Pharaoh would not listen, and the next day, the land was filled with the sound of mourning. Now the Egyptians couldn't get rid of the Hebrews quick enough.

The Plagues

Do you know anyone who is stubborn and wants to get his or her own way, no matter what? Have you ever been like that? The trouble with stubborn people is that they usually end up hurting not only themselves but others too.

Pharaoh was definitely a stubborn man. On top of that, he was very proud and thought he was more important than anyone else—even God. Moses told him again and again that he must let God's people leave Egypt. Each time Pharaoh said no. And each time, God sent yet another terrible plague. Pharaoh's stubbornness hurt the people of Egypt, the animals, and even himself.

The opposite of being stubborn and proud is being humble. It means putting God and others first—as Jesus always did. God can help you to be like that too!

Dear God, please forgive me for the times when I am stubborn. Help me always to follow and obey you. **Amen.**

Reflection Questions

1. Have you ever been stubborn? Why is it sometimes so hard to obey—whether it's obeying God or your parents or your teachers?

2. What does putting others first mean to you? What does putting God first mean?

Action Points

1. When are you most tempted to be stubborn? Is it when you're with a certain person or when you're asked to do a certain chore? Make a plan now for how you will choose to be humble in that situation.

2. Think of the chore you least like to do. Now, surprise your parents by doing it—before they even ask you to.

CROSSING THE RED SEA
Exodus 14–15

The Hebrews travelled across the desert towards the Red Sea. But Pharaoh regretted his decision and set off with his army to bring them back. Soon the people were trapped between the sea and the Egyptians, but Moses told them, "God will look after us."

Then God told Moses to raise his staff and stretch out his hand over the sea to divide the water so that the Israelites could go through the sea on dry ground. A column of cloud moved between the Hebrews and the Egyptians so that the Egyptians could not see what was happening. Moses stood before the sea and raised his hand, and all that night the Lord drove the sea back with a strong east wind and turned the seabed into dry land. The waters were divided, and the Israelites went through the sea on dry ground with a wall of water on their right and on their left!

Crossing the Red Sea

Have you ever had a problem so big, you thought there was just no way to solve it? That's definitely what the Israelites thought! They were trapped between the Red Sea on one side and the Egyptian army on the other. But Moses reminded them of this very important truth: When you look to God, he'll take care of you. That's when a miracle happened. The wind blew and the waters parted—and God's people walked right through the middle of the sea on dry ground!

You may not be trapped between an ocean and an army, but you might feel trapped by a problem, a worry, or a fear. That's when you need to look to God. Love him, trust him, do what he says is right—and God will rescue you too.

> **Dear God,** sometimes my troubles seem so very big. Help me remember that you are bigger and you will always help me. **Amen.**

Reflection Questions

1. Is there a problem you're facing? Write it out and then talk to God about it. He'll help you find the answer.

2. It's important to take time to talk to God every day—whether you're struggling with a problem or not. Write down a plan for when and where you will talk to God each day. And then get started on that plan today.

Action Points

1. You can be the answer to someone else's problem. Is there someone who needs a friend or an older neighbour who could use a helping hand? Do one thing each day to help someone else.

2. Is there someone who has helped you? Write a letter telling that person thank you. Then deliver it with a smile, a hug, and maybe a cookie or two.

THE TEN COMMANDMENTS

Exodus 19–20

Moses led the people to Mount Sinai. There God spoke to Moses and told him that if the people would honour and obey him, then he would always be with them. The elders agreed to do everything the Lord had told them. Then God told Moses that in three days he would appear to them on Mount Sinai.

On the morning of the third day, there was thunder and lightning, with a thick cloud over the mountain and a loud trumpet blast. The people trembled and waited at the foot of the mountain. Then God called Moses to the top of it and spoke to him, saying: "I am the Lord your God, who brought you out of Egypt.

"You shall have no other gods before me.

"You shall not make any false idols.

"You shall not misuse my name.

"Remember the Sabbath and keep it holy.

"Honour your father and your mother.

"You shall not murder.

"You shall not commit adultery.

"You shall not steal.

"You shall not tell lies.

"You shall not envy anything that belongs to your neighbour."

Moses told the people what God had commanded, and they promised to obey.

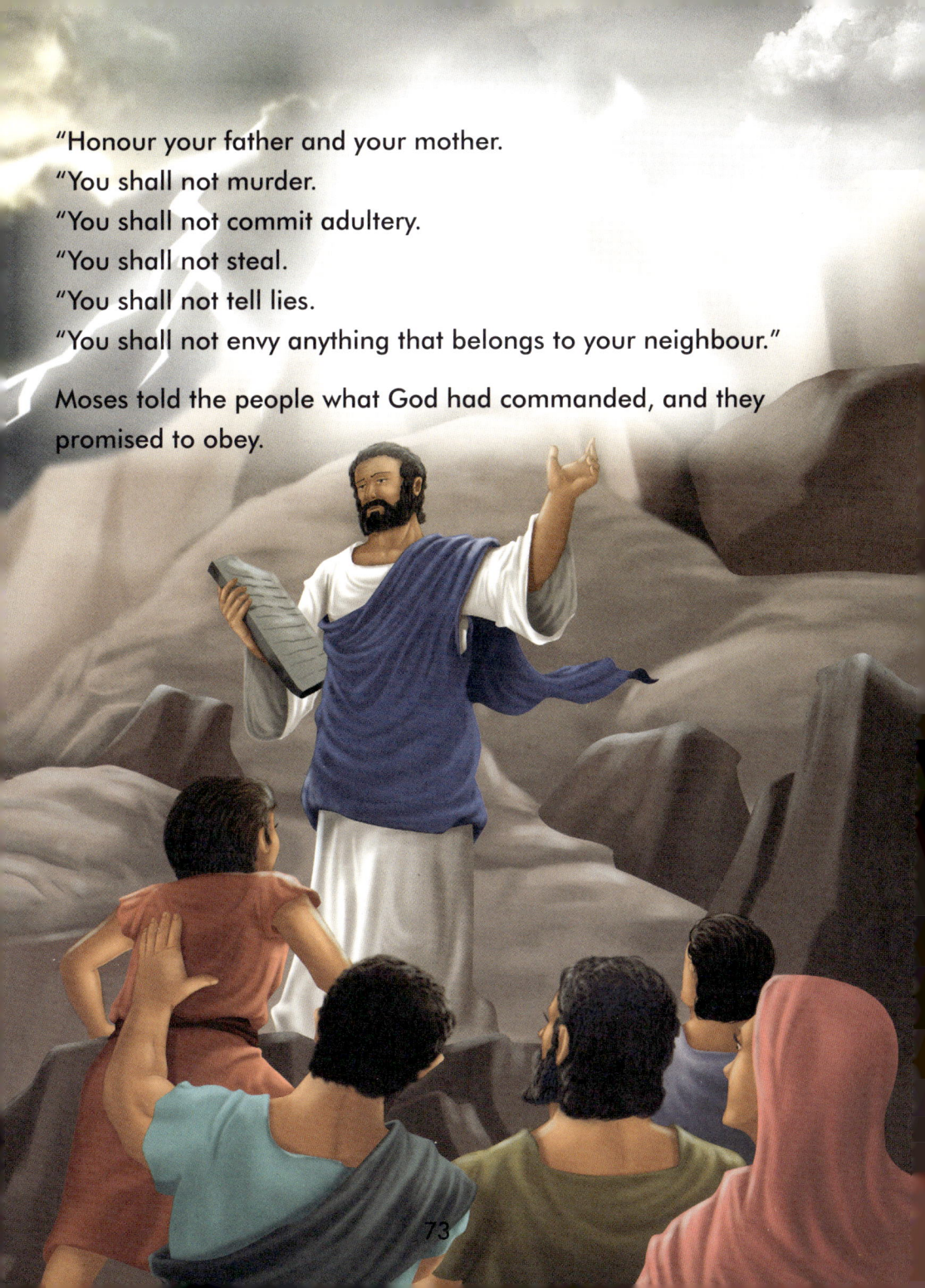

The Ten Commandments

Rules are everywhere. There are rules at school, like don't push and shove in line. There are rules at home, like keep your toys off the stairs and don't hit your brother. And there are even rules in the car, like always wear your seat belt. Some people think rules are about taking away their fun. But that's not true! Rules are made to keep you safe and to help you treat others right.

When God gave Moses the Ten Commandments, it wasn't to take away your fun either. Just like the rules of this world, God's rules keep you safe and help you treat others right. Most of them seem like common sense now—of course we shouldn't lie, steal, or kill—but when they were first given, they helped God's people to live in a wonderful new community that was like no other on the earth.

Dear God, thank you for giving me rules to live by. And thank you for sending Jesus so that I can be forgiven when I forget to follow your rules. **Amen.**

Reflection Questions

1. Is there a rule you really don't like? Take some time to think about that rule and write it down. Now think about why it might have been made. How might it help you or keep you or someone else safe?

2. If you could make up any rule, what would it be? Why would you make that rule? How does it help people or keep others safe?

Action Points

1. Write out the Ten Commandments, but put them in your own words. Add some art and then post them somewhere you'll see them every day.

2. The first four of the Ten Commandments teach us how to love and worship God. Take some time to tell God how much you love him. You can do it with a picture, a prayer, or a song.

THE GOLDEN CALF

Exodus 32

Moses spent many days on the mountain. Eventually, the people began to believe he would never come back down. They asked Aaron to make them gods to lead them. Aaron told them all to gather their gold jewellery and used it to make a beautiful golden calf, which he placed on an altar.
The people gathered round and began to worship it.

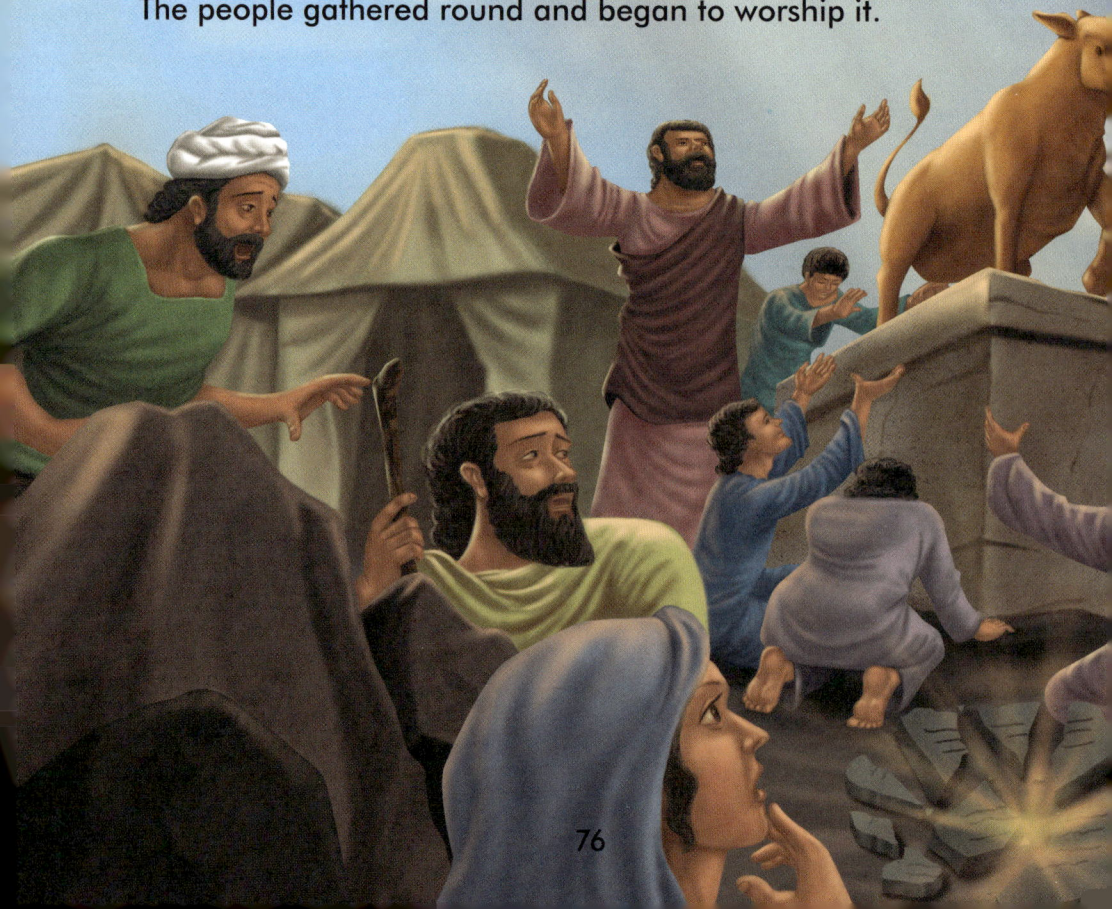

God was angry with them and vowed to destroy them, but Moses pleaded with him to forgive them, and God relented.

Then Moses went down from the mountain with the tablets. When he saw the people singing and dancing around the golden calf, he was so furious that he threw the tablets to the ground, where they shattered. Next he burned the calf and ground it to powder. God punished those who had sinned with a plague.

The Golden Calf

Do you ever think, "I wish I could go to the match instead of church"? Or "I'd rather watch television than read my Bible"? Of course, there's nothing wrong with sports matches or television. But when you start choosing those things over God, that's when they can cause a problem—an idol problem. An idol is anything that becomes more important to you than God.

The Israelites had an idol. It was a golden calf, and they worshipped it instead of God. But that golden calf didn't rescue them from Egypt or part the Red Sea or send them manna from heaven to eat. Only God could do those things, and only God can work in your life. Don't let any kind of idol—not friends or hobbies, television or money—come between you and God. Only God is worthy of your worship.

Dear God, please show me anything that
I have made more important than you.
Help me to worship only you. **Amen.**

Reflection Questions

1. The Israelites' idol was a golden calf. List some idols people worship today with their time and money and attention.

2. You probably don't have a golden calf in your room, but are there things—friends, sports, hobbies—that you make more important than God? List a few, and ask God to help you put him first.

Action Points

1. What can you do today to show God how important he is to you? You might draw a picture, write a song, or simply spend time talking to him.

2. Make a list of all the wonderful things around you that God created. Could an idol create any of those things? Praise God for being so powerful, so mighty, and so amazing!

WATER FROM THE ROCK
Numbers 20

God told Moses that he and his people must now travel to the land God had promised them. The people soon began to grumble, for they were in the desert without water. Moses and Aaron asked God to help. "Speak to that large rock before their eyes," God replied, "and it will pour out water."

Moses and Aaron gathered the people. "Listen, you rebels, must we bring you water out of this rock?" Moses said, then struck the rock twice with his staff. Water gushed out, and everyone was able to drink.

But God was disappointed because Moses hadn't followed his instructions, nor had he given the credit to God. So he told the brothers that they would never enter the Promised Land.

Water from the Rock

When you're thirsty, what do you? Perhaps you get a drink from the fridge. Or maybe you ask your teacher if you can get a drink from the water fountain. But would you ever ask a rock to give you a drink? Of course not! Why? Because there's no water inside a rock. There's just more rock!

But when the Israelites were thirsty in the desert, God didn't tell Moses to go to the nearest fridge or water fountain. He sent Moses to a rock. God is so powerful and so amazing that he can even get water from a rock. The next time you're thirsty, take a minute to remember how the Israelites got their water from a rock—and then praise God for being so amazing!

Dear God, you are so powerful and so amazing. I am grateful that you love me. **Amen.**

Reflection Questions

1. The New Testament says the Israelites "drank from the spiritual rock...and that rock was Christ" (1 Corinthians 10:4). In what way is Jesus like the rock in this story?

2. Another part of this story tells us that God was angry because Moses said he (Moses) got the water out of the rock. Why would this make God angry?

Action Points

1. It can be hard for homeless people to find clean water to drink. Ask your parents if you can keep bottles of water in your car to give to the homeless people you see.

2. You can be thirsty for water, but you can also be thirsty for God's Word. Read John 4:4-26. What do you think Jesus meant by "living water"?

THE WALLS OF JERICHO
Joshua 6

After many years, the Israelites finally reached the Promised Land, and the first city they laid siege to was Jericho. God told Joshua, "I have delivered Jericho into your hands. March around the city once with all the armed men.

"Do this for six days. Have seven priests carry trumpets in front of the Ark of the Covenant. On the seventh day, march around the city seven times with the priests blowing the trumpets. When you hear them sound a long blast on the trumpets, have all the people give a loud shout. Then the walls of the city will collapse, and Jericho will be yours."

For six days the Israelites marched around the city just as God had told them, and on the seventh day, they marched around Jericho seven times. On the last time, when the priests sounded the trumpet blast, Joshua commanded the people, "Now shout! For the Lord has given you the city!"

When the trumpets sounded, the people raised a mighty cry, and the city walls trembled and then collapsed before them! The soldiers charged in and took the city. Only a woman named Rahab and her family were spared, for the city and everything in it was burned, except for the silver, gold, bronze, and iron.

And the story of how the Lord had helped Joshua take Jericho spread throughout the land!

The Walls of Jericho

Have your parents ever asked you to do something that just doesn't make sense? Like make your bed—when you're just going to mess it up again at the end of the day! When your parents ask you to do something you don't understand, it's still important to obey them. Obeying shows that you love and respect them.

Sometimes, God asks his people to do things that don't make sense. Think about Joshua. Who would have thought that marching around Jericho would do any good? But Joshua loved God and trusted him, so he obeyed him, and Jericho's walls went tumbling down. When God asks you to do something you don't understand—like love your enemies or be kind to the bully at school—be like Joshua. Obey God because you love him, and he'll do awesome things in your life!

Dear God, I don't always understand the things you ask me to do, but I will trust you. Help me to obey you always. **Amen.**

Reflection Questions

1. Is there something your parents or teachers ask you to do that just doesn't make sense? Why might they ask you to do it?

2. Jesus often did things that the world said didn't make sense—like eating with sinners, touching people with leprosy, and talking to Samaritans. Why do you think Jesus did those things?

Action Points

1. Defeating Jericho was a big challenge for Joshua and the Israelites. Think of a big challenge facing you, and ask God how he wants you to overcome it.

2. The Bible says, "Do everything without grumbling or arguing" (Philippians 2:14). Decide today that you will obey—even if it doesn't make sense—without grumbling or arguing. Choose to smile instead.

GIDEON AND THE THREE HUNDRED

Judges 7

God chose Gideon to free his people from the Midianites, who bullied them. The Israelites assembled a large army, but the Midianite army stretched as far as the eye could see. Even so, God said to Gideon, "You have too many men. I do not want the Israelites to think they have won because of their own strength. Tell anyone who is afraid that he can go home."

After Gideon had spoken to his army, only 10,000 remained! But God said, "You still have too many men. Tell them to go and drink from the water, and take with you only those who cup the water in their hands to drink, not those who lap it." When this was done, only 300 men were left!

That night Gideon looked down on the sea of tents. How could they ever win? God knew he was anxious and told him to creep down to the enemy camp, where he overheard the soldiers recounting bad dreams about losing! He returned full of confidence and roused his men, giving them all trumpets and empty jars with torches inside.

The men reached the edge of the camp and, following Gideon's signal, they all blew their trumpets, smashed the jars, and shouted out loud. The harsh noise and sudden light startled the Midianites so much that the camp fell into confusion, and the soldiers fled in terror, even fighting one another in their fright!

In this way, Gideon and God defeated the Midianites with just 300 men!

Gideon and the Three Hundred

Have you ever looked at a problem and thought, "There's just no way I can fix this. I can't do it." That's what Gideon thought. He and the Israelites had been ready to fight the massive army of the Midianites. That is, until God kept sending groups of Gideon's soldiers home. Soon, he had only 300 soldiers left! What could Gideon and 300 soldiers do against thousands and thousands of armed Midianites? Not a thing—by themselves. But they weren't alone. God was with them.

Gideon trusted God, and God fixed Gideon's problem. And God will do the same for you. When you face a problem that's just too big to fix on your own, trust God. Follow him, and he'll give you a way to fix it.

Dear God, thank you for always being ready to help me. I know there's no problem you and I can't handle together. **Amen.**

Reflection Questions

1. How might Gideon and his soldiers have felt when God sent them into battle against such a huge army? Have you ever felt that way? When?

2. How might Gideon and his men have felt after defeating the Midianite army? Have you ever felt that way? When?

Action Points

1. Make a reminder for yourself to trust God like Gideon did. Write the words of Proverbs 3:5-6 on a poster or piece of paper. Then place it where you'll see it each day.

2. Gideon couldn't take credit for his victory—it was clearly a miracle. Think of some ways you can give God credit for the things he's done for you and through you.

SAMSON AND DELILAH

Judges 16

❧❦❧

Samson was a thorn in the side of the Philistines. Although he never led an army, he carried out many attacks against them. But when he fell in love with Delilah, a beautiful Philistine woman, they bribed her to find out the secret of Samson's strength.

Night after night Delilah would plead with Samson to tell her his secret. In the end, he finally told her: "If anyone were to cut my hair off, then I would lose all my strength." When Samson awoke, it was to discover that the Philistines had come into his room and cut off his hair. Now he was powerless as they bound and blinded him and threw him into prison!

Over time, Samson's hair grew back. One day, the Philistine rulers were all gathered for a feast in a crowded temple. Samson was brought out to be made fun of. He was chained between the two central pillars of the temple. Then Samson prayed to God with all his heart: "Give me strength just one more time, my Lord, so that I can take revenge upon my enemies!"

Once more Samson was filled with strength. He pushed against the pillars with all his might, and they toppled. The temple crashed down, killing everyone inside. Samson killed more of his enemies with this final act than he had killed in all of his life!

Samson and Delilah

Has your mum or dad ever said to you, "If you make good choices, I will be able to trust you and give you permission to do fun things"? That's great! But have they ever said, "When will you learn to make the right choice?" Oh, that's sad, because there are consequences for bad choices.

Samson had a super strong body, but one thing he was weak about was making the right choices. One day he made a bad choice. He told somebody a secret when he shouldn't have. God couldn't trust Samson and gave him a big time-out in jail.

God wants us to make good choices all through our lives. He gave us the Bible so we could know what he wants us to choose. Good choices mean God can trust us and give us the best rewards.

Dear God, thank you for the Bible, which tells us how to make good choices. I want to do the right thing and cooperate with you. **Amen.**

Reflection Questions

1. Think of a good (but difficult) choice you have made. How did you feel after you made that good choice?

2. Write down a few good choices you already know God wants you to make.

Action Points

1. Is there a good choice you often struggle to make? Talk with your parents about why it's so hard and how you can make it easier to choose well.

2. Make a sign that says, "I will choose to do the right thing today." Put it where you can see it first thing in the morning.

FAITHFUL RUTH
Ruth 1–4

Naomi was moving back to Bethlehem. Her husband and sons had died, and she wanted to go home. But she begged her beloved daughters-in-law, Orpah and Ruth, to stay behind, for she was penniless, and her life would be hard.

Orpah and Ruth loved Naomi dearly and did not want to stay behind, but finally Orpah agreed to go home. Loyal Ruth, however, said, "Don't ask me to leave! I will go wherever you go. Your people will be my people, and your God will be my God."

So it was that Ruth and Naomi came to Bethlehem. Soon they had no food left, and brave Ruth went out into the fields, where workers were harvesting the crops, and asked the owner if she could pick up any of the barley that his workers left behind.

This man was Boaz. He kindly let Ruth work in his fields and told his servants to share their food with her. When Ruth returned with a full basket of food, Naomi knew that the Lord was looking after them, for Boaz was a relative of hers. In time, Ruth married him, and when they had a son, there was no happier woman in the whole of Bethlehem than Naomi!

Faithful Ruth

Everybody loves to be with kind people. Kind people think about what makes others happy. They take care of others when they are sick or hurt. Do you have a kind friend? Can you count on that friend to always be ready to help you? Be happy if you have one or two friends who are both kind and faithful.

Ruth was a friend to Naomi. She stuck with Naomi when they travelled to Bethlehem because they were hungry. She went out in the fields to pick up leftover grain they could grind into flour and make into bread. She listened when Naomi gave her instructions, and she did exactly as she was told. And because she was kind and faithful, God rewarded her.

God wants us to have kind and faithful friends, and he wants us to be kind and faithful to others. Are you a kind friend?

Dear God, thank you for my kind and faithful friends. Help me to be the same kind of friend to them and to others. **Amen.**

Reflection Questions

1. Have you ever seen other kids bully someone? That surely is not kind. How did you feel when you saw that?

2. One of the kindest things we can do is to pray for our friends. The Bible tells us to "pray for each other" because "the prayer of a righteous person is powerful and effective" (James 5:16). Whom can you pray for today?

Action Points

1. Make a prayer journal by folding two regular sheets of paper in half to form a book. Decorate the cover any way you like. Inside, write the names of friends you want to pray for and what you are praying for them, like this: "Sammy—I pray he will get better grades in maths."

2. Set a time every day to pray for your friends. Be faithful to prayer.

DAVID AND GOLIATH
1 Samuel 17

Young David stood before Goliath. Mighty Goliath was the fearsome champion of the Philistine army, and he was so big and powerful that he was practically a giant! Goliath had challenged the Israelite soldiers to fight him one-on-one. Not one of them had dared to face this terrible warrior, but David did. God had been with him when he had protected his sheep from lions and bears, and David knew that God would be with him now.

The king gave David his own armour and weapons, but they were too big and heavy for the young boy. So David stood before Goliath with nothing but his staff, a sling, and five smooth stones from a nearby stream.

Goliath laughed when he saw the young shepherd boy, but David fearlessly ran towards him, putting a stone in his sling and flinging it with all his might. It hit Goliath in the middle of his forehead. When he fell to the ground, David raced up and, drawing out Goliath's own sword, cut his head from his body with one stroke!

The Philistines were so shocked when they saw their champion killed that they turned and ran away!

David and Goliath

Want to know something really cool? When God asks you to do something, no matter how hard it might seem, you can do it! Other people may say you can't do whatever it is God wants you to do, but they are wrong. And God will help you. He wants us to depend on him. So if he asks you to stand up to a bully, you can do it. If God wants you to tell the truth when others are lying, you can. If God asks you to put extra money in the collection plate, do it because he will make sure you have enough money for everything you need.

God knows you are stronger and braver than you think you are. He also promised he will never leave you, so when you go to do the right thing, God is beside you, helping you and making you strong.

Dear God, help me remember you are always beside me. When you ask me to do something, I believe you will make me a warrior as mighty as David. With your help, I can do whatever you ask me to. Thank you for that! **Amen.**

Reflection Questions

1. Wow, David was really brave...or was he? What are some of the emotions you might have had if you were the one facing Goliath?

2. Goliath wasn't impressed with David's weapons—a sling and a few stones. What surprising "weapons" has God given you? (Check out Matthew 5:44 for a couple of ideas.)

Action Points

1. Think about something you are being asked to do that you think is too hard for you. Write it down. Then write: "I can do all this through him who gives me strength" (Philippians 4:13).

2. Creating a plan of action sometimes makes doing a hard task easier. Write out two or three steps to begin your work.

GOD'S PROMISE TO DAVID

2 Samuel 7; 1 Chronicles 17

O ne day King David called the prophet Nathan to him. "It does not seem right that I am living in such a splendid palace, while God's covenant chest is in a makeshift tent. I want to build a fine temple for it!"

That night God spoke to Nathan. In the morning, the prophet told the king, "God has always travelled with his people in a tent, to be with them wherever they went. He does not want you to build him a temple."

David was bitterly disappointed, but Nathan continued. "God does not want you to build him a house, for it is he who will build a house for you. It is because of him that you left your sheep and fields to become king of all Israel. He promises that he will be with you and help you overcome your enemies. With his guidance, you will become the greatest king upon earth, and your sons will be kings of Israel after you forevermore."

David was filled with gratitude. When Nathan had gone, David gave his thanks to God in a heartfelt prayer. He had wanted to do something for God, but God had done something wonderful for him, a simple shepherd boy, instead.

God's Promise to David

Nobody likes to hear the word no, especially when we really want to help someone—maybe even God. Sometimes when God says no, we don't understand. Sometimes it's our parents who say no. We argue and beg, trying to change the no to yes. Parents work hard to decide what is best for us, and sometimes they can't let us do what we want. When we hear no, we must admit that not doing what we wanted might be best for us.

King David thought he had a great idea—to build a beautiful house for God. But God said no. And it wasn't, "No, wait a while." It was just plain no. Then God promised David that he would always be with him and help him and that David would become a great king. David made the right choice to obey God, and so can you.

Dear God, I don't like to hear someone say no when I ask for permission to do something. But I know that you love me and that the reason you say no is to protect me. **Amen.**

Reflection Questions

1. Think of a time when you wanted to do something and your parents told you no. Write down how you felt.

2. Have you ever prayed and prayed and prayed for something and it didn't turn out as you hoped? Why might God have said no?

Action Points

1. When we don't get an answer to a prayer, or when we don't get the answer we wanted, we must continue praying. If you made a prayer list earlier, look at it and pray again for some unanswered prayers.

2. When God said no to David, he gave David some tremendous promises. List some of the awesome blessings in your life, and thank God for each one.

GOD SPEAKS TO SOLOMON

1 Kings 3; 2 Chronicles 1

Soon after David's son Solomon had been crowned king, God spoke to him in a dream. "What would you like me to give you, Solomon?" he said. "Ask for whatever you want."

Solomon answered, "I am young and have no experience of ruling a nation. I would ask you to give me wisdom that I might rule over your people wisely and do as you would have me do. Help me to distinguish between what is right and what is wrong."

God was pleased with Solomon's answer. "Most people would have asked for wealth, or long life or great victories," he said. "You have asked only to be wise. I will give you wisdom. But I will also give you those things you did not ask for. You will be rich and respected, and if you follow in my ways, you will live a long and good life."

When Solomon awoke, he felt comforted and strengthened knowing that God was by his side.

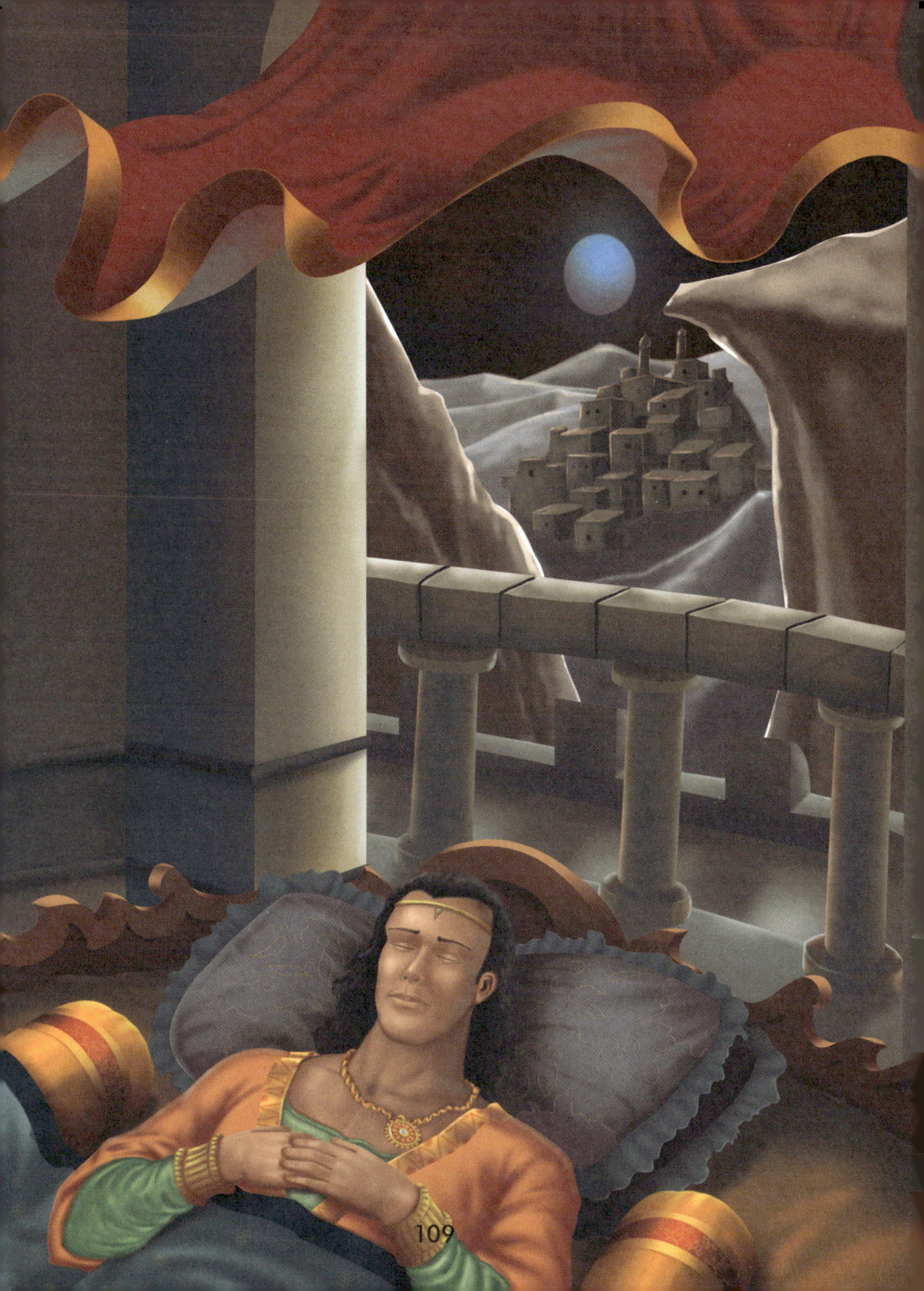

God Speaks to Solomon

Imagine going to bed tonight and hearing God ask you in a dream, "What can I give you?" What would your answer be? Would you ask for a lot of money? For good friends? A healthy body? An awesome ability?

When God asked King Solomon what he could give him, Solomon told God he wanted to be wise. What does "wise" mean? Well, it's more than having lots of information. Wisdom doesn't come from books.

Wisdom comes from making good decisions and especially from learning from the Bible. People who are wise make the best decisions. They choose to do what God wants them to.

God tells us to ask for wisdom. He wants us to be wise, and when we are, we will live long, happy lives.

> **Dear God,** please help me to make good decisions and gain more wisdom every year. Thank you. **Amen.**

Reflection Questions

1. Whom do you know who is wise? Is it a grandparent? Your priest? A teacher? What made you think of that person?

2. What situations in your life might be easier to face if you had more wisdom? Whom can you talk to about them?

Action Points

1. It's not too early in your life to begin asking God to make you wise. Some boys and girls are very wise for their age. So start praying for wisdom.

2. Most people who are wise think for a while before they give advice. The next time someone asks you what you think, don't answer right away. Try to figure out what is the best action to take. That's the wise thing to do.

THE FIERY FURNACE
Daniel 3

W hen Israel was in exile in Babylon, King Nebuchadnezzar had a huge statue built and told the people to worship it or they would be thrown into a blazing furnace. Shadrach, Meshach, and Abednego refused, saying, "Your Majesty, we will not bow down to anyone but our God. He can save us from the furnace, but even if he doesn't, we will never worship your statue."

The angry king told his guards to tie them up tightly with ropes and to stoke up the furnace until it was seven times hotter than usual. Then they were thrown into the flames. The furnace was so hot that the guards themselves were scorched to death!

Nebuchadnezzar looked on. Suddenly, he leaped up in disbelief, for within the furnace he could see four men. Shadrach, Meshach,

and Abednego were no longer bound but walked around freely, and with them was a fourth man who looked like the Son of God!

The king called to the men to come out of the fire, and the friends walked from the flames unharmed. Their skin was not burned, and their clothes were not singed. Nebuchadnezzar was amazed. "Your God is indeed great, for he sent an angel to rescue his servants who were willing to give up their lives to follow his commands. He should be praised. No other god could do as he has done!"

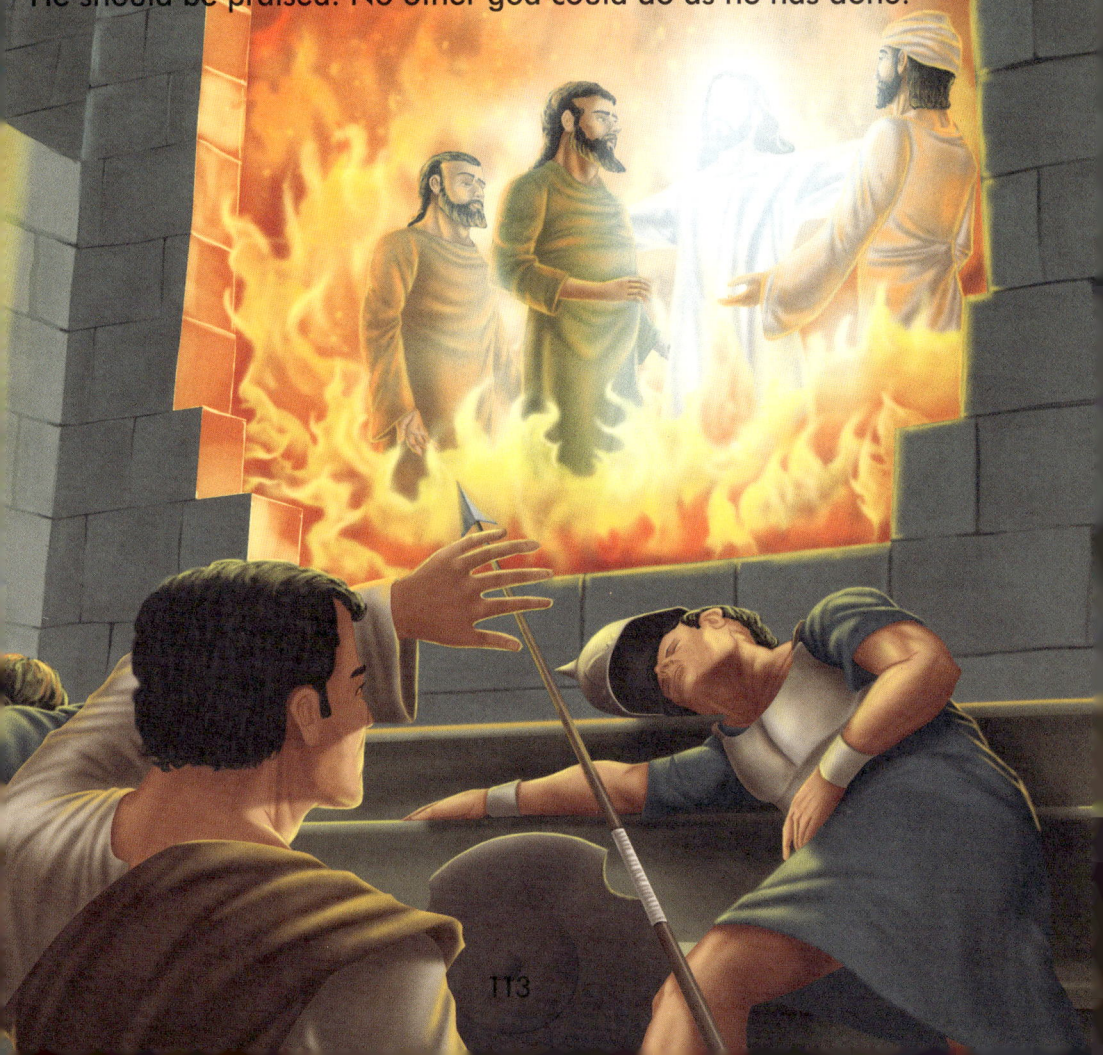

The Fiery Furnace

Sometimes even when we are doing everything right, some really scary bad things can happen. Maybe we get hurt or sick. Maybe someone we love moves away. Maybe a pet gets injured. God said, "I'll never let you down, never walk off and leave you" (Hebrews 13:5 MSG). Because we believe in Jesus, we will never be alone. Never! Not ever! At no time! No matter what happens, Jesus has promised to be with us.

That's the same lesson Shadrach, Meshach, and Abednego learned when a very angry and wicked king tossed them into a fire. They were probably so scared they could hardly stand up. But the minute they were inside the fire, they discovered someone was with them who looked like the Son of God. He was right there in the worst situation ever—and he rescued them.

He is with us in our most difficult situations too.

Dear God, I'm so glad to learn that you are always with me no matter what happens. Next time I start to panic, I'll remember and thank you for being with me. **Amen.**

Reflection Questions

1. What is the worst situation you have ever been in? As you picture the scene, add Jesus into it…because he really was there. What might he have said to you?

2. What do you think Shadrach, Meshach, and Abednego might have said when they came out of the fire?

Action Points

1. Draw a picture of you doing something that is hard or scary. Then add Jesus to the picture to help you remember he is always there.

2. Tell someone you know what you have learned about Jesus's promise never to walk off and leave you.

YOUR NAME IS WONDERFUL!

Psalm 8

Oh, Lord, how wonderful is your name!

Your glory shines down from heaven;
it is seen everywhere on earth.
The praise of young children
silences your enemies and makes you strong.
When I think about how you made the heavens,
how you placed the moon and stars in the sky,
I wonder how you can care about human beings—
we are so small!

Yet you have made us only a little lower than the angels.
You have made us rulers over everything you created:
the birds and the beasts, the fish in the sea.
We rule over all of them.

Oh, Lord, how wonderful is your name!

Your Name Is Wonderful

Regardless of how old you are, you can praise the Lord. God loves to hear the praises of children. Jesus even said, "Let the little children come to me" (Matthew 19:14). Jesus loves kids.

What can we say when we praise God? For a start, we can praise him for the stars and the moon that light up the night sky. We can praise him for the sun that gives us warmth and light. Each heavenly body has its own place in the universe, and nothing bumps into anything else. Then we can praise him because he made us—kids and grown-ups—and he watches over every one of us. We can also praise God because he put us in charge of everything on the earth.

Best of all, we can praise him for always loving us and making it possible for us to live with him forever. He is an awesome God!

Dear wonderful, powerful, mighty God, I love you and I praise you. Help me to praise you every day. **Amen.**

Reflection Questions

1. Some people never take the time to praise God. What can you do to motivate yourself to praise God every day?

2. We praise God with our words but also with our actions. In what ways can you bring God glory today?

Action Points

1. Make a praise card and put it where you can see it every day. A praise card can have a pretty design or picture that you make. You can write, "Today I praise God for [fill in the blank]."

2. When we share our praises for God with others, we encourage them to praise God too. Tell a parent or a brother or sister or a friend what you praise God for today.

THE LORD IS MY SHEPHERD

Psalm 23

The Lord is my shepherd;
he will make sure I have everything I need.
He lets me rest in green meadows.
He leads me beside quiet streams to drink.
He refreshes my soul.
He shows me the right way to go,
so that I can bring honour to his name.
Even though I walk through the darkest of valleys,
I will fear nothing, for you are with me;
your rod and your shepherd's crook make me feel safe.
You prepare a feast for me in front of my enemies.
You anoint my head with oil;
I feel so honoured that I am overwhelmed.
Surely your goodness and love will be with me
every day of my life,
and I will live in the house of the Lord forever.

The Lord Is My Shepherd

If you were a sheep, what would you need? Food, water, protection, a place to hide from danger, someone to tend to your wounds, someone to find you when you are lost…

We are not sheep, but we need many of the same things they do. God said he is our shepherd. He will take care of us and provide everything we need. He can heal us when we are sick, and he stays close by when we are scared.

What do you need today? Is there trouble in your family that you would like God to fix? Maybe your family needs money. God cares when there isn't much money, and when we pray, he helps us. Is someone in your family sick or sad? God, our shepherd, cares for the sick and the brokenhearted. And if you are ever scared, you can remember he is always nearby.

Dear God, sometimes I get scared about things. I'm glad you are right beside me so I can tell you all the things I need. I'm glad you hear. **Amen.**

Reflection Questions

1. Write down a few things you would like God, your shepherd, to do for you today.

2. Write down a few things God might like for you, one of his sheep, to do today.

Action Points

1. Now begin to pray about what you wrote. Sometimes it helps to write out our prayers.

2. Read Psalm 23 in your own Bible.

A LAMP FOR MY FEET

Psalm 119

How blessed are they who are good,
who follow the ways of the Lord
and seek him with all their heart.

But how can young people keep their lives pure?
By obeying your commands.
I seek you with all my heart
and love your laws.
Please give me understanding
and keep me strong
that I may follow your laws.
Your words taste sweet in my mouth;
they are a lamp for my feet,
a light on the path on which I travel.
You are my refuge and my shield.
I put all my hope and trust in you.
Steady me with your hand
and help me to honour you.
I am like a sheep that was lost.
Please come and look for me,
for I remember all your commands.

A Lamp for My Feet

Have you ever gone outside at night, maybe to take out the rubbish or bring in the dog? Some nights have moonlight, but other nights are very dark, and it's hard to see. At your house you probably know where the rubbish bin is, and if you call the dog, he will come. So you do okay at home. But what if you were in a place where you had never been before? You would need a light to find your way around.

Sometimes we just don't know which way to turn. We don't know what's right and what's wrong. God gave us a gift to help us. His Word, the Bible, is the light we need to show us how to behave and think. We need to read the Bible every day. If you come across something you don't understand, ask a grown-up or a big sister or brother to help you.

Dear God, thank you for giving us a light, your Word, to show us the way to live and to remind us of your love. I love your Word. **Amen.**

Reflection Questions

1. God's Word shows us how to live, so why do you suppose so many people never read it?

2. Do you ever wonder what to do—what is the best decision to make? Write down a decision you're facing, and ask someone to help you find out what the Bible has to say.

Action Points

1. Look up these verses in the Bible. Like a lamp, they will guide you and help you know what is right about…

   - Cursing and swearing: Exodus 20:7
   - Stealing: Exodus 20:15
   - Obeying your parents: Colossians 3:20
   - Being kind: Ephesians 4:32
   - Going to church: Hebrews 10:25

2. Make a Bible-reading plan today. Choose a special spot to sit, a time to read (usually either the morning or the evening), and how much you'd like to read. (One chapter? Five minutes?) Your parents can help you find a Bible-reading plan online that suggests specific Bible readings for each day.

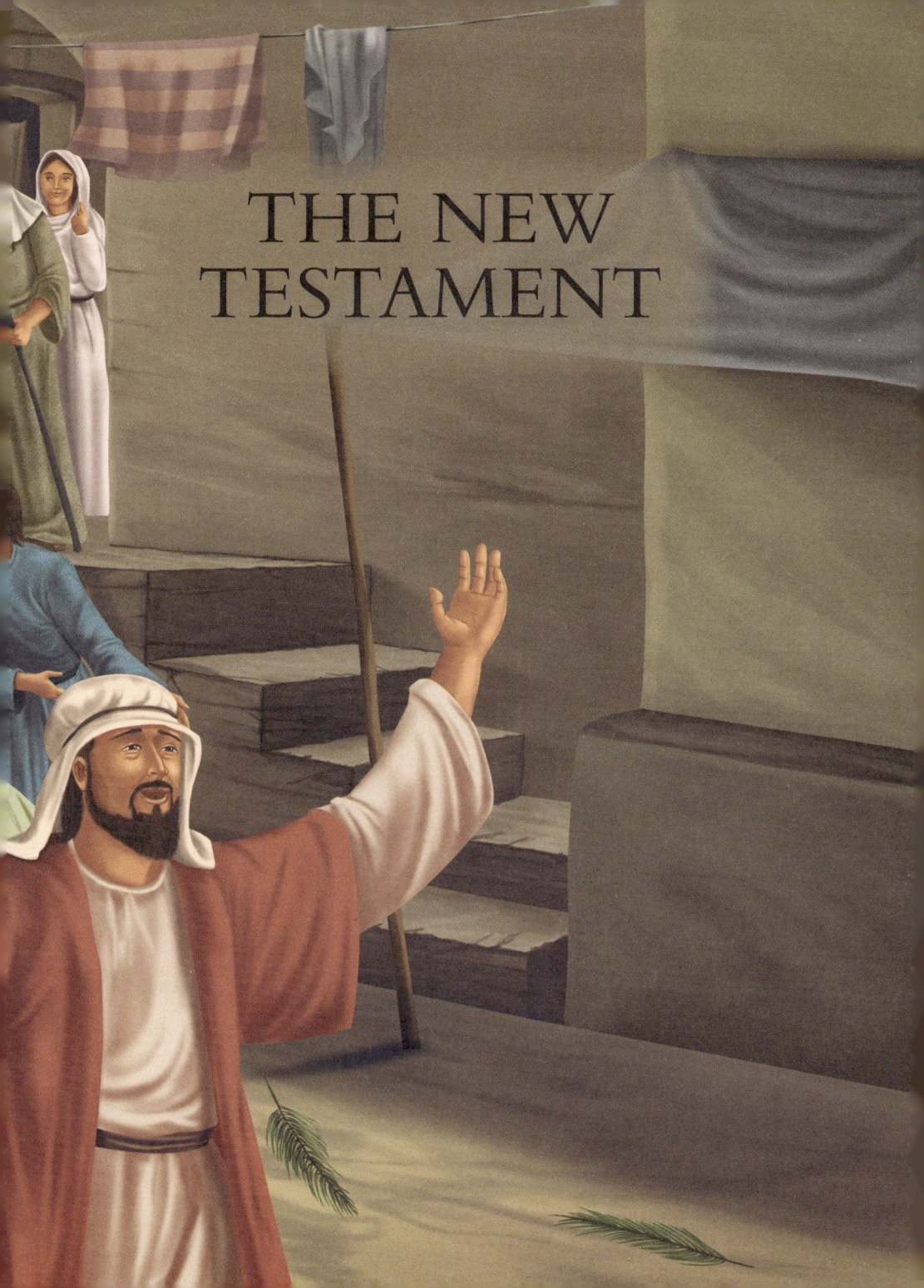

THE NEW TESTAMENT

THE HOLY LAND
IN THE TIME OF JESUS

The Great Sea
(Mediterranean)

Sidon

Tyre

PHOENICI

GAI

Caper

Beths
Cana

Mt Carmel ▲

Nazareth

Nain

Caesarea

SAMARIA

Samaria

Shechem
(Sychar)

Ephrain

Jerich

Emmaus

Jerusalem ▲ Mt of

Beth

Bethlehem

JUDEA

IDUMEA

ABILENE

Damascus

SYRIA

Caesarea Philippi

TETRARCHY OF
PHILIP

hsaida Julias

f Galilee

DECAPOLIS

ura

NABATEA

MARY IS CHOSEN BY GOD

Luke 1

God sent the angel Gabriel to the house of Mary in the town of Nazareth in Galilee. Mary was engaged to Joseph, a carpenter who could trace his family all the way back to King David.

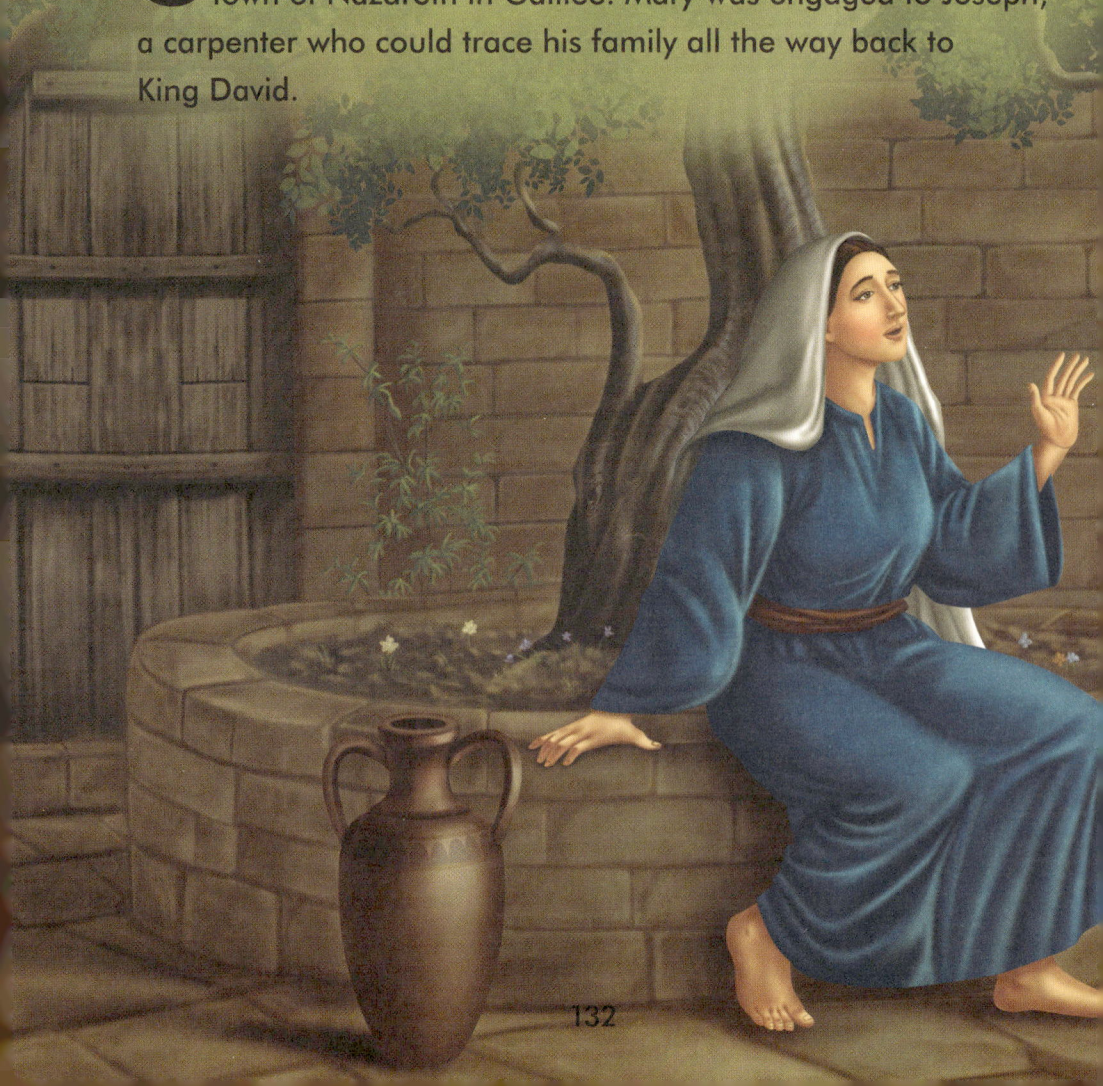

"Do not be afraid, Mary," the angel told the startled girl. "God has chosen you for a very special honour. You will give birth to a son, and you are to call him Jesus. He will be called the Son of God, and his kingdom will never end!"

Mary was filled with wonder. "How can this be?" she asked softly. "I am not even married!"

"Everything is possible for God," replied the angel. "The Holy Spirit will come on you, and your child will be God's own Son."

Mary bowed her head humbly, saying, "It will be as God wills it."

Mary Is Chosen by God

When your parent asks you, "Will you pick up the toys in your room?" or "Will you take out the rubbish?" it's up to you to decide whether you will do it. Of course, refusing usually brings a consequence.

Mary, the mother of Jesus, was probably not expecting anything special to happen the day an angel suddenly appeared and said she would be the mother of Jesus the Messiah. This was big news! Mary had a choice. She could say, "No, I don't want to do it. Go away, angel." Or she could say, "Yes, I will do what you ask." She chose to do as God asked. Mary was willing to do something hard when God chose her.

Someday God may ask you to do something very hard. What do you think you will say? Are you willing to do whatever he asks?

Dear God, help me to be as willing as Mary to say yes to you. I don't know what you will want me to do, but I want to be ready and willing. **Amen.**

Reflection Questions

1. How might you be able to tell whether God is asking you to do something?

2. List a few things you've wondered if God is asking you to do. (You don't have to be sure!)

Action Points

1. God talks to kids as well as grown-ups. Next time you think God is speaking to you, write down what you believe he is saying.

2. Choose an adult to talk with about this. Ask them if they believe God speaks to them. Share what you believe God is saying to you.

JESUS IS BORN
Luke 2

Around this time, the emperor of Rome ordered a census of all the people he ruled over. All the people throughout the lands ruled by Rome had to go to their hometown to be counted.

Mary and Joseph had to travel to Bethlehem, the town of Joseph's ancestor David. By the time they arrived, they were tired and desperately wanted to find a room for the night, for it was clear that the time had come for Mary's baby to be born. But the town was filled to bursting. Every inn was full!

At last, an innkeeper showed them to a stable, and there Mary's baby was born. She wrapped him in strips of cloth, then laid him gently on clean straw in a manger. Mary and Joseph looked down upon their son with joy, and they named him Jesus, just as the angel had told them to.

Jesus Is Born

Have you ever been super excited about something but also really nervous at the same time? That's how Jesus's parents must have felt as they travelled to a faraway place with a baby due to arrive any day. When they got to the inn and found out they would have to sleep in a stable, they must have been so disappointed.

But the thing is, God had a big plan that was set in place long before Mary and Joseph were born. Their obedience to him allowed that plan to happen. They got to meet Jesus! So when you face disappointments, feeling excited but nervous, remember that God has a plan for your life too!

Dear God, thank you for planning great and wonderful things in my life, and help me to be patient through the disappointments I face. **Amen.**

Reflection Questions

1. When were you really disappointed by something? How did you feel?

2. What helped you feel better when things didn't go the way you thought they would?

Action Points

1. Write this on a card and put it somewhere you'll see it every day: "God has great and wonderful plans for me."

2. Next time your mum or dad says no to something you want, take a deep breath and just say, "Okay, thanks." See what happens!

THE SHEPHERDS' STORY

Luke 2

That same night, an angel appeared to some shepherds in the hills above Bethlehem. As they fell to the ground in fear, the angel said, "Do not be afraid. I bring you good news. Today in the town of David a Saviour has been born to you; he is the Messiah, the Lord. Go and see for yourselves. You will find him wrapped in cloths and lying in a manger." Then the sky was filled with angels praising God!

When the angels had left, the shepherds
hurried to Bethlehem where they found
the baby lying in the manger just as
they had been told. And when
they had seen him and knelt
before him, they rushed off to tell
everyone about this special baby
and the wonderful news!

141

The Shepherds' Story

Have you ever seen something totally amazing? Maybe it was a double rainbow in the sky or a lion roaring at the zoo. When we experience something really cool, we just have to tell other people about it. We can't keep it a secret.

That's how the shepherds must have felt the night Jesus was born. Not only did angels sing to them while they were out in the fields working, but they also had the chance to go and meet Jesus—the actual, real Jesus—in person. Wow! They probably never forgot that night, and they probably told the story to everyone they met for the rest of their lives.

Dear Father, you are amazing, powerful, and glorious. The shepherds got to see that for themselves. I can't wait to see you in person too. **Amen.**

Reflection Questions

1. What's something totally amazing you've experienced?

2. How do you think the shepherds felt when they saw the real baby Jesus?

Action Points

1. Tell someone what you find amazing and exciting about Jesus today.

2. Write down ten things that are awesome about God. Ask your parents to help you if you need to!

"MY FATHER'S HOUSE"

Luke 2

When Jesus was about 12 years old, his mother and father took him to Jerusalem to celebrate the Passover—the festival which reminded the Jews of how God had rescued them from slavery in Egypt so many years before. For one whole week the city was filled to bursting.

At the end of this time, Mary and Joseph set off for home with a group of other people, but on the way they realised Jesus was missing. Frantic with worry, they rushed back to the crowded city to search for him. At last, on the third day of searching, they found him in the temple courts talking with the teachers of the Law, who were amazed by how much he knew.

"Jesus!" cried his parents. "We've been so worried about you!"

"But why were you looking for me?" answered the young boy. "Surely you knew that I would be in my Father's house." For while Jesus loved Mary and Joseph dearly, he understood that God was his Father in a very special way.

"My Father's House"

Jesus was just 12 years old when he amazed the teachers (called rabbis) at the temple with how much he knew. Why? It was because he loved the Lord more than anything. That made him want to learn as much as he could about God.

Of course, we know Jesus was God's Son, but he was also fully human. He was truly just a boy. You are a child too, and if you really want more than anything to learn about God's ways, you can learn from God's Word, just as Jesus did. God is more than happy to teach you all about himself.

Father, give me the ability to understand what the Bible is saying so that the more I read it, the more I will understand and know you. **Amen.**

Reflection Questions

1. If your parents lost track of you at a big gathering, where might they find you playing?

2. Do you think a child can learn the Scriptures the way an adult can?

Action Points

1. Commit to reading one Bible story every day.

2. Write down your favourite Bible verse, and tell your parents why you love it so much.

TESTED IN THE DESERT
Matthew 4; Mark 1; Luke 4

Jesus was baptized, and then he spent 40 days and nights in the desert. He ate nothing and was desperately hungry. The devil came to him and said, "If you are the Son of God, surely you can do anything. Why don't you tell these stones to become bread?"

Jesus answered calmly, "It is written: 'Man shall not live on bread alone, but on every word that comes from the mouth of God.'" Jesus knew that food wasn't the most important thing in life.

The devil took Jesus to the top of the temple and told him to throw himself off, for surely angels would rescue him. But Jesus said, "It is also written: 'Do not put the Lord your God to the test.'"

From a high mountain the devil offered him all the kingdoms of the world if Jesus would simply bow down and worship him. But Jesus replied, "Away from me, Satan! For it is written: 'Worship the Lord your God, and serve him alone.'"

When the devil realised that he could not trap Jesus, he gave up and left him, and God sent his angels to Jesus to help him recover.

Tested in the Desert

Saying no to temptation can be really hard. Maybe your mum or dad has said no to screen time, period. But then you are at a friend's house, and they start playing video games. Your mum will never know…should you play too?

You know the right answer, but it's hard, isn't it? While Jesus was in the desert, Satan tempted him with things he could easily have wanted, such as bread and the chance to be a king. But Jesus kept his eyes focused on what God, his Father, said to him through Scripture. That is how he was able to keep from giving in to temptation.

Dear Father, please help me to say no to Satan when he tempts me. **Amen.**

Reflection Questions

1. Why do you think God allowed Jesus to be tempted like this?

2. What gave Jesus the strength to say no to temptation?

Action Points

1. What are three things you can do to stay strong when you're tempted?

2. Sometimes a thing that's normally fine to do (like eating bread) can be a temptation for someone. How can you be sure not to tempt your friends, as in the video game story above?

DEMONS AND HEALING
Matthew 8; Mark 1; Luke 4

Jesus was preaching in a town in Galilee. The people were amazed. They were used to listening to the teachers of the Law, but Jesus was different. He seemed to speak with real authority. In the synagogue, there was a man who had an evil spirit in him. Jesus ordered the spirit to come out of the man, and it did. News about what happened quickly spread.

Later, Jesus went to the home of Simon Peter and Andrew. Simon Peter's mother-in-law was ill in bed, but Jesus gently took her hand and helped her sit up.

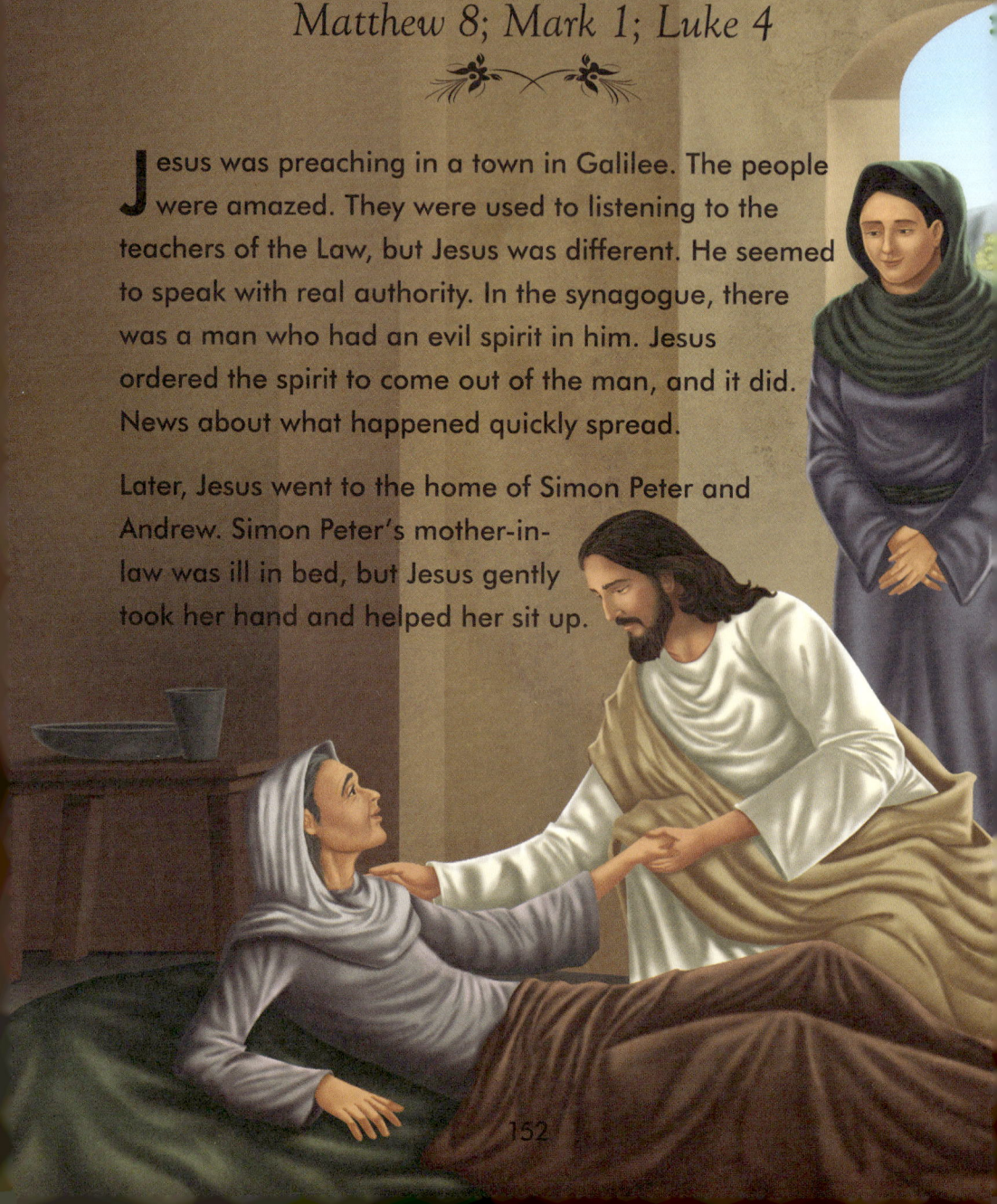

Instantly, she felt better. "I should be looking after you,"
she smiled at Jesus, and she jumped straight out of
bed and began to get dinner ready.

News of her wonderful recovery spread like wildfire,
and by evening a large
crowd gathered outside. People
had brought loved ones or had
come themselves to be healed.
And Jesus went out to them.

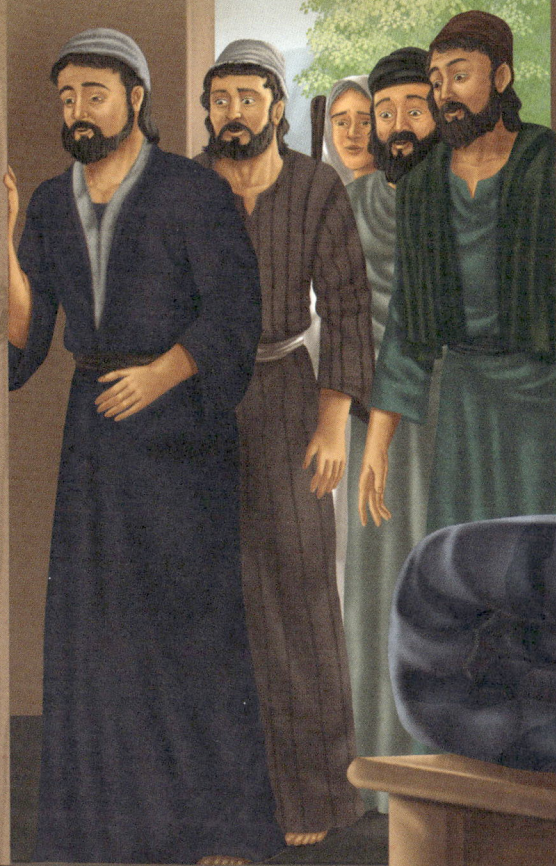

Demons and Healing

You know what it's like to feel sick, don't you? Your body hurts, and you are tired and probably a little cranky. Everything just feels wrong, and you want to feel better.

Jesus cares about all of that. He spent a lot of time during his ministry on earth making sure people felt better whether they were sick in their bodies or sick in their hearts. He paid attention, loved them, and healed them. And that is a glimpse of what life forever in Jesus's kingdom will be like.

Dear God, thank you for helping me to feel better when I am sick. I love you, Father. **Amen.**

Reflection Questions

1. What's the worst thing about feeling sick?

2. Why do you think Jesus dislikes it when people are sick?

Action Points

1. List a few things you can do to help someone who is sick to feel a little better.

2. Think of someone who may not feel good—in their body or their heart—and do something simple to improve their day.

JESUS AND THE
TAX COLLECTOR
Matthew 9; Mark 2; Luke 5

Matthew had a well-paying job as a tax collector, but when Jesus told him to follow him, he gave up his job on the spot. He wanted all his friends to meet Jesus too. But when the Jewish religious leaders learned that Jesus was meeting with tax collectors and sinners, they were disgusted. "Why is he mixing

with the likes of them?" they asked one another. "Everyone knows that tax collectors are greedy and dishonest!"

But Jesus told them, "If you go to a doctor, you don't expect to see healthy people. It is people who are sick who need to see the doctor. I am God's doctor. I have come here to save those people who are sinners and want to start afresh. Those who have done nothing wrong don't need me."

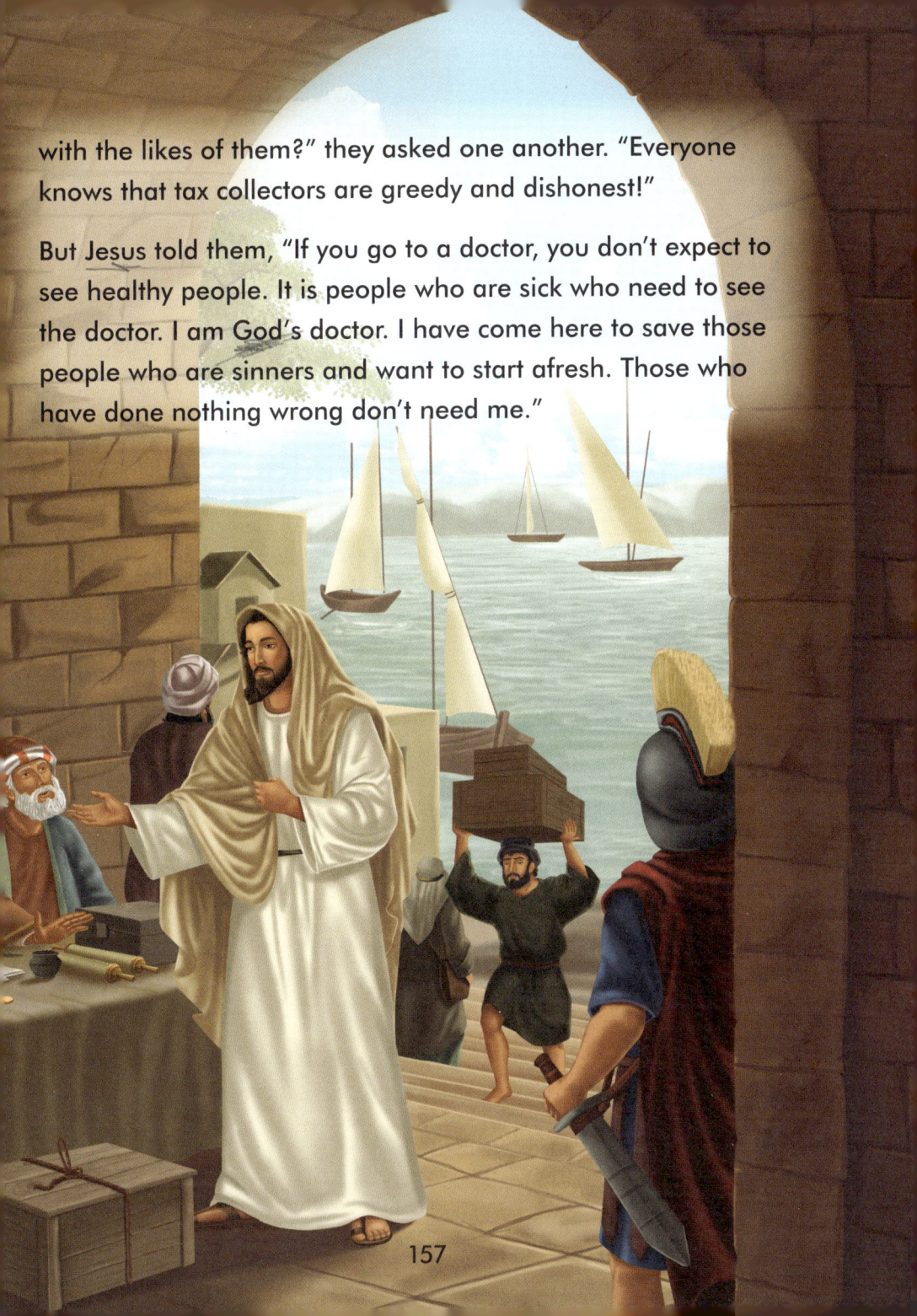

Jesus and the Tax Collector

Have you ever felt as if you needed to be perfect in order for God to love you? Maybe you've thought that before you become a Christian, you need to have everything figured out. No more arguing or leaving your room messy or refusing to eat vegetables at dinnertime.

Jesus told us he came so he could show sinners (like you and me) that God loves them just as they are. He welcomes them into his new family, and *then* they can start leaving their sinful ways behind. There is no need to have it all figured out on your own. In fact, that is impossible, which is why Jesus came in the first place.

Thank you, God, for loving me
so much just as I am. **Amen.**

Reflection Questions

1. What's your most embarrassing habit?

2. How does it make you feel to know Jesus loves you even though you are not perfect?

Action Points

1. Tell Jesus you are so thankful he came to save us while we were still sinners.

2. Tell one person today Jesus loves us even though we aren't perfect yet.

THE UNHOLY TEMPLE
John 2

Jesus and his followers went to the temple in Jerusalem to pray. But when Jesus entered, he was appalled, for it was full of moneylenders and people selling animals. It looked more like a marketplace than a holy temple! Jesus was furious. He drove the animals out of the temple and knocked over the tables of the moneylenders. "Get out!" he shouted. "How dare you turn my Father's house into a marketplace? Be gone!"

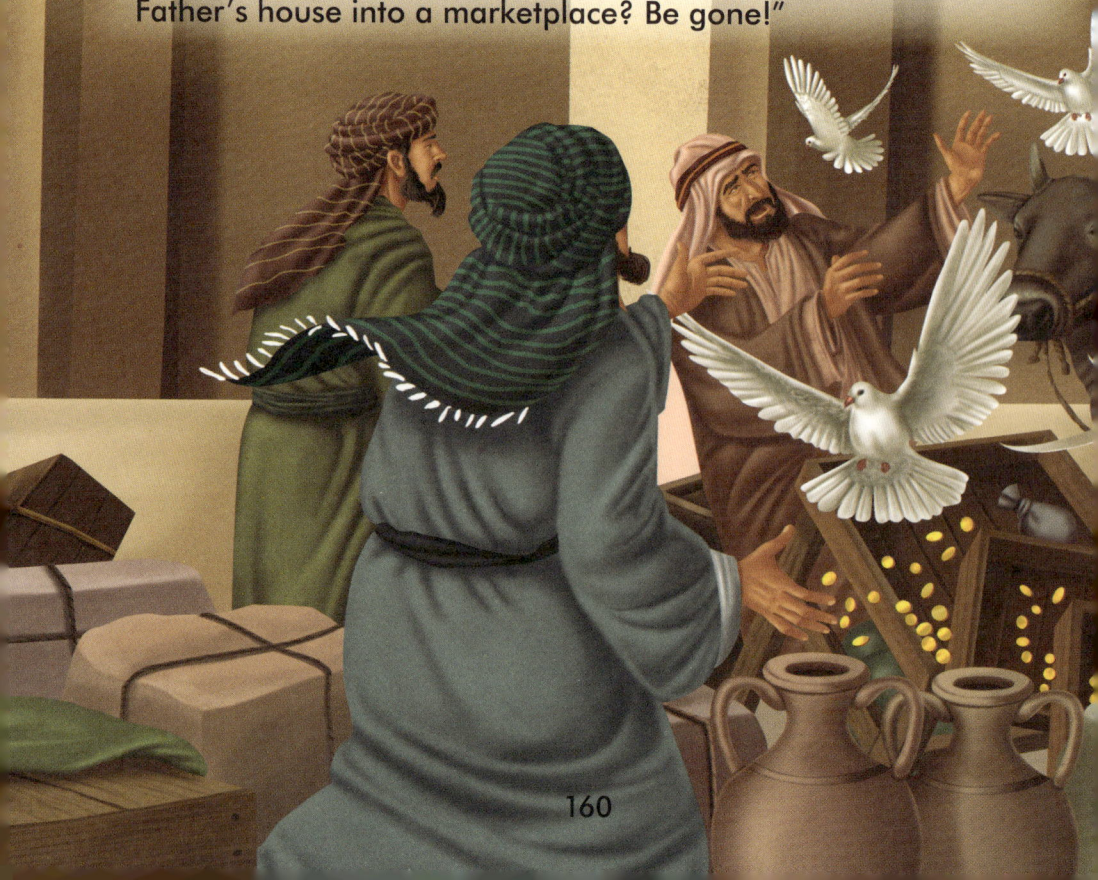

When the temple was quiet and peaceful once more, Jesus began to teach his followers about God's kindness and mercy. Many of the priests and leaders were jealous of Jesus and wished to stop him, but they couldn't do anything because the people paid attention to what Jesus said and listened to him.

The Unholy Temple

The most amazing, wonderful, unbelievable thing about God's grace is that it is completely free. We don't have to do anything to earn it. So when Jesus saw people in the temple—his Father's own house!—charging people money to be forgiven, he was angry. Really angry.

It's okay to be angry when people are not being treated fairly or right. But remember, after Jesus kicked out the greedy people, he told everyone there about God's free gift of grace so they could receive it too.

Thank you, Father, for your wonderful and free grace. I am so happy to be your child. **Amen.**

Reflection Questions

1. How do you feel when you read about Jesus being strong and defending the temple and the poor people?

2. Have you ever been angry because another person was being mean? If so, when?

Action Points

1. If someone you know is being treated badly, what is one thing you can do to help them?

2. Write down three things that are good about having a God who defends the weak.

THE VISITOR AT NIGHT

John 3

❧ ⚜ ⚜ ❧

Nicodemus was one of the Jewish leaders. He was impressed by Jesus but didn't want anyone to know, so he went to speak to Jesus late at night when he would not be seen. He said he knew Jesus had been sent by God because of the wonderful miracles he had performed.

But Jesus was not impressed with flattery. "No one can see the kingdom of God unless they are born again," was all he said. This confused Nicodemus, who couldn't understand how an old person could be born again.

Then Jesus replied, "Unless you are born of water and the Spirit, you cannot enter the kingdom of God." And when Nicodemus still did not understand, Jesus continued: "The Son of Man must be raised up so that whoever believes in him may have eternal life. For God so loved the world that he gave his only

Son, so that those who believe in him should not perish but have eternal life. For God sent his Son into the world not to condemn it, but so the world might be saved through him."

Jesus was talking about a spiritual birth, not a physical birth—one that would come about by believing in Jesus himself.

The Visitor at Night

Being "born again" is something you will hear Christians talk about a lot, but it is a confusing thing to say, isn't it? Even Nicodemus, a grown man, did not understand what Jesus was talking about. So here is what it means.

Even though a baby's life actually starts way before he is born, we still say, "This is the first day of his life!" on the day he is born. It is the first day of his life outside the womb. Just like that, when a person becomes a Christian, we say, "This is the first day of your life with Jesus." It is as if they were born…again!

Dear God, thank you for the chance to be born twice—once as a baby and again as your child. I love you, Father. **Amen.**

Reflection Questions

1. Have you been born again? If so, when did that happen? If not, whom can you ask to help you be born again?

2. Why is it important for a person to get a fresh start in their new life with Jesus?

Action Points

1. Thank Jesus for giving you a chance to be born again into a friendship with him.

2. Ask two people today what they think being born again means.

JUST SLEEPING
Matthew 9; Mark 5; Luke 8

Jairus was desperate! His little girl was dreadfully ill, and he was worried that Jesus wouldn't be able to make his way through the crowds to heal her in time. Then Jesus stopped still and asked who had touched him. "Master, everyone is touching you in this crowd!" said a disciple, but Jesus knew that he had been touched in a special way.

As he looked around, a woman stepped forward and knelt at his feet. "Lord, it was me," she said nervously. For years she had been ill, and nobody had been able to help her, but she had known that if she could just get close to Jesus, she would be healed. Sure enough, the moment she had managed to touch the edge of his cloak, she was well!

Jesus wasn't angry. "Woman," he said kindly, "your faith has healed you. Go home now."

Just then they were told that Jairus's daughter was dead! Jairus was heartbroken, but Jesus continued walking. "Trust me, Jairus," he said. He arrived at the house to the sound of weeping. "Why are you carrying on so?" Jesus asked. "The girl is not dead; she is just sleeping." He went to her room, where he took one of her hands in his own and whispered, "Wake up, my child!"

In that instant, the child opened her eyes. She smiled at Jesus and hugged her overjoyed parents!

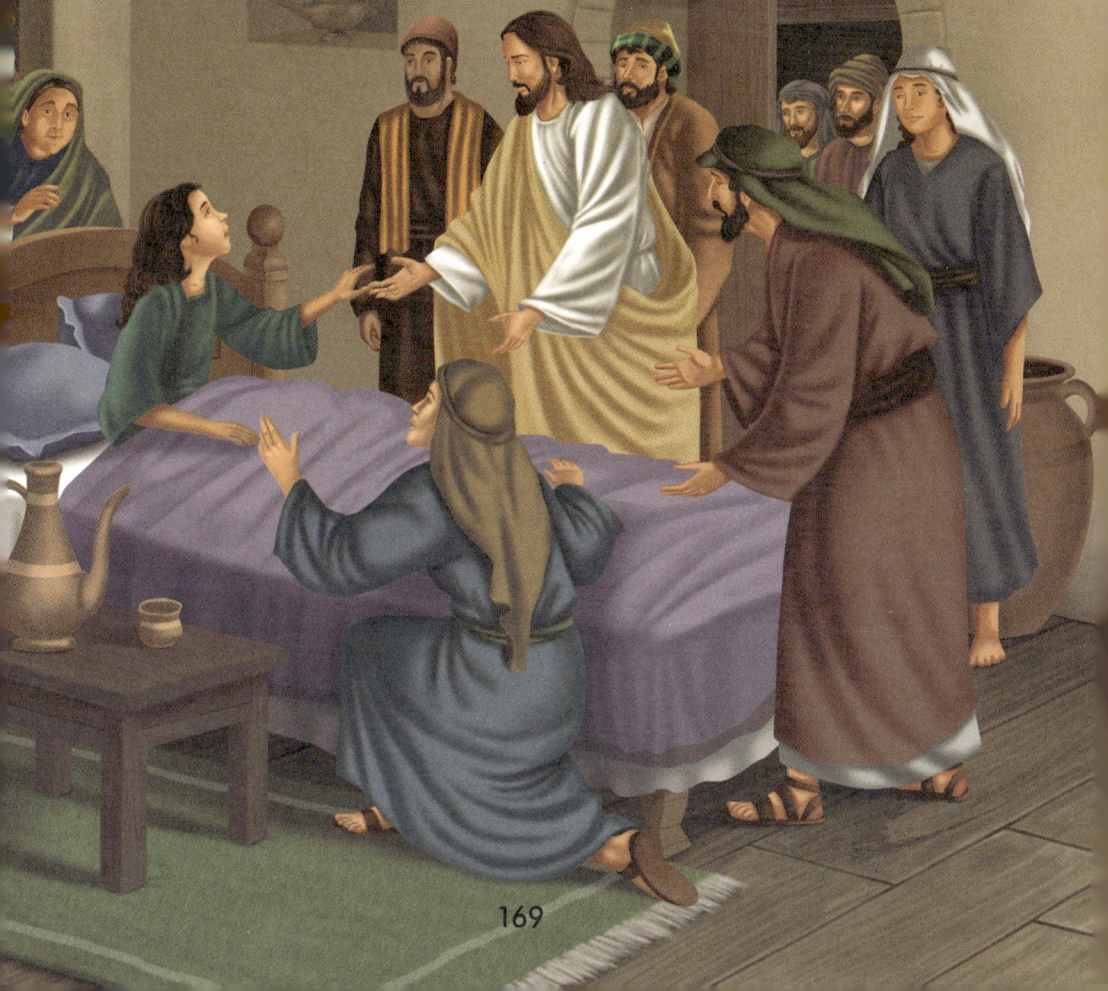

Just Sleeping

Have you ever wanted something so much you felt worried it would be gone and you wouldn't get to have it unless your parents hurried to the shops to buy it? Your heart was probably beating fast, and your hands were nervous. You just wanted to get it *now*!

Imagine how Jairus felt, knowing his daughter was really sick and Jesus was the only one who could heal her. But the crowds were making Jesus walk slowly. Of course, Jesus wanted to help as many people as he could, including Jairus's daughter…and you. Jairus was worried, but Jesus wasn't.

What problem do you want him to help you solve? Remember, he is powerful enough to raise a person from the dead. He is happy to listen to your worries too.

> **Father in heaven,** thank you for helping me with things too big for me to handle on my own. **Amen.**

Reflection Questions

1. How does it make you feel to know that Jesus is so powerful?

2. What worries do you want to tell Jesus about?

Action Points

1. Write down your worries on a piece of paper or draw a picture of them. Then crumple it up and put it in the bin to show you have given those worries to Jesus.

2. Write Jesus a thank-you note for loving you enough to care about the things that worry you.

SERMON ON THE MOUNT
Matthew 5; Luke 6

Jesus wasn't always welcome in the synagogues, so he would often teach his disciples and the large crowds which gathered outside in the open air. One of the most important talks he gave was on a mountain near Capernaum. It has become known as the Sermon on the Mount. Jesus taught the people about what was truly important in life and gave comfort and advice:

172

"How happy are the poor and those who are sad or who have been badly treated, those who are humble, gentle and kind, and those who try to do the right thing—for all these people will be rewarded in heaven! They will be comforted and know great joy. Those who have been merciful will receive mercy, and God will look kindly on those who have tried to keep the peace, for they are truly his children. So be glad when people are mean to you and say nasty things about you because of me—for a great reward is waiting for you in heaven!"

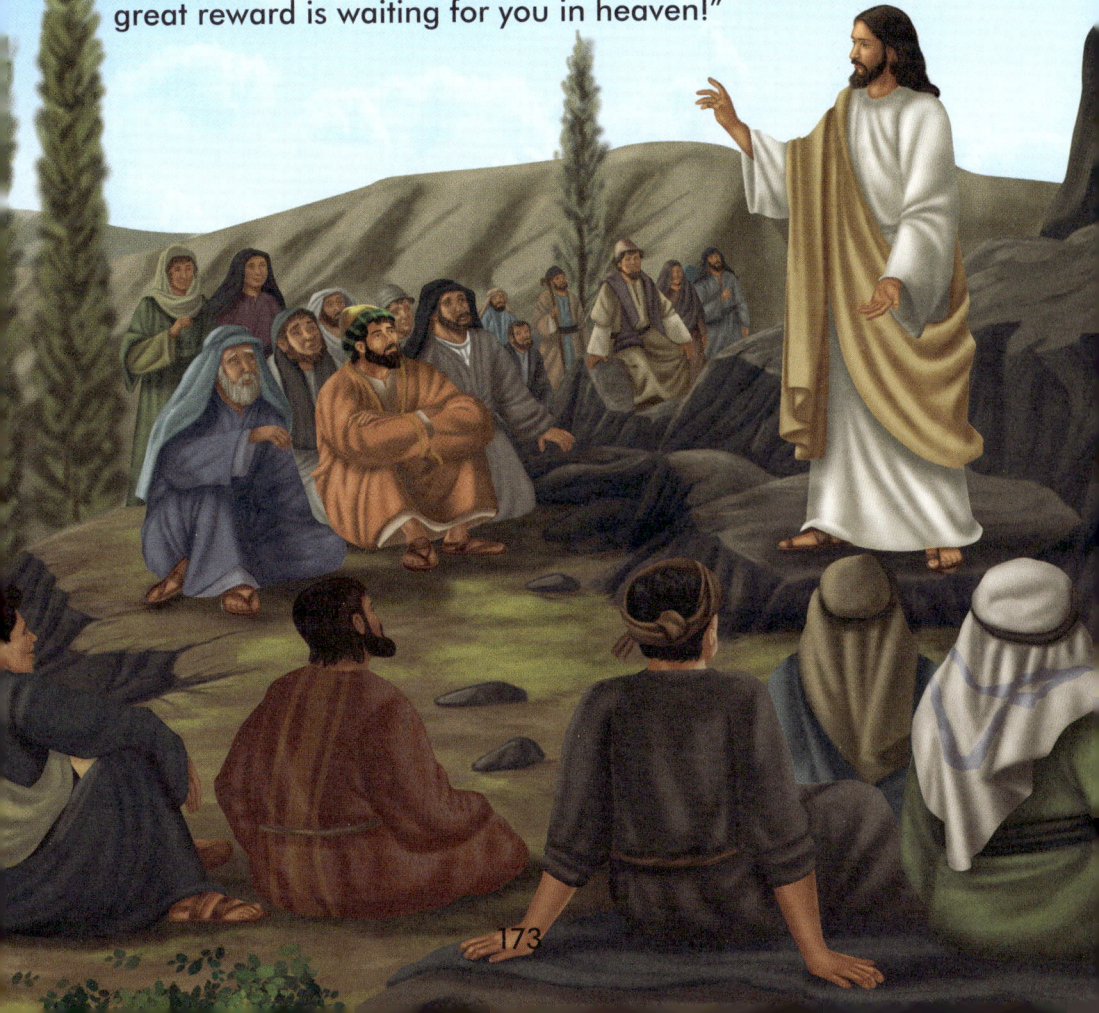

Sermon on the Mount

If you could have just one thing in life to make you happy, what would it be? A new video game system? A better bike? Those things would be really fun, but what Jesus says will actually make us happy is surprising.

Jesus said people who are kind, who do not argue with their friends or family, and who are teased for being Christians are the ones who will be happy. Why? Because of the amazing rewards God has planned for them in heaven. So next time you are *dying* for the newest, coolest thing around, take a minute first to ask Jesus how important it should be to you.

Dear Father, help me to want what is really important in life, not just things that seem cool. **Amen.**

Reflection Questions

1. Why would being sad or teased be something that could make you happy?

2. Why is being a peaceful person who does not argue or fight with others so important to Jesus?

Action Points

1. Find three to five good toys in your room you can donate to someone who doesn't have any toys. Notice how it makes you feel to give them to someone who needs them.

2. Make a promise with your siblings or friends to go for one whole week without any fighting.

A FIRM FOUNDATION
Matthew 7; Luke 6

Before Jesus ended his sermon, he said one last thing: "If you listen to my teaching and follow it then you are wise, like the person who builds his house on solid rock. Even if the rain pours down, the rivers flood, and the winds rage, the house won't collapse for it is built on solid rock. But he who listens and doesn't obey is foolish, like a person who builds a house on sand, without any foundation.

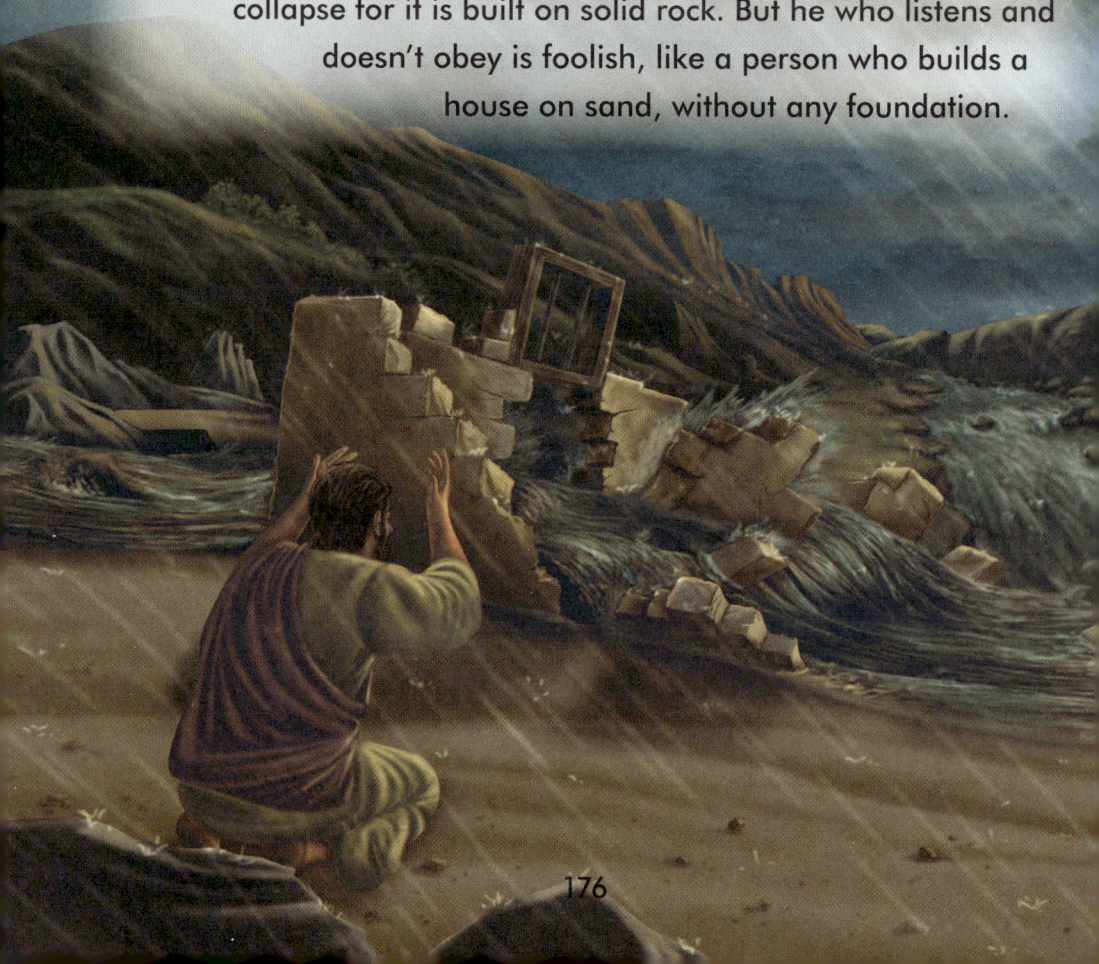

"The house is quickly built, but when the rains and floods and winds come, the house will not be able to stand against them. It will collapse and be utterly destroyed."

As the crowds slowly dispersed, their heads were filled with all these new ideas. Jesus was nothing like their usual teachers, but what he said made sense. There was much to think about!

A Firm Foundation

For fun, let's try different word pictures to make the same point Jesus did in this parable. Have you ever heard someone start a project by saying, "Let's get this off on the right foot"? Maybe your teacher wants to start the school year off right. So she tells you what she expects, making everything clear "from square one." ("Right foot" and "square one" express the same idea as setting a firm foundation.)

Years ago, kids played a game called hopscotch. What might have happened if they had hopped with their left foot instead of their right in square one? They might have lost their balance or even stumbled or hopped out of bounds.

In this parable we read Jesus's guidelines for setting a firm foundation: listening to and following his teaching. These are his requirements for getting us off on the right foot in our Christian lives—from square one.

> **Dear Lord,** thank you for making what you expect so clear. Thank you for offering your Word and example to guide us. **Amen.**

Reflection Questions

1. When we have a firm foundation, the storms of life won't overwhelm us. What "storms" (or difficulties) have you or your family faced?

2. How can your family continue to build a firm foundation—one that's built on Jesus's teachings?

Action Points

1. List some of the items that describe your family's foundation—things about your family that help you to feel safe and secure.

2. Using dice or other small objects that don't link together, build a pretend house on a plate and another one in a bowl filled with dry cereal. Walk around with each one to see which house stays up the longest.

JESUS CALMS THE STORM
Matthew 8; Mark 4; Luke 8

Jesus and his disciples climbed into a boat to travel across to the other side of the lake. Jesus was so tired that he lay down and fell asleep. Suddenly, the skies darkened, rain came pelting down, and a fierce storm struck the lake. Huge waves tossed the boat, and the disciples were terrified that they would capsize.

Jesus still lay sleeping. The frightened disciples went over and woke him up, begging him to save them. Jesus opened his eyes and looked up at them. "Why are you afraid? You have so little faith!" he said sadly. Then he stood up calmly, his arms spread wide, and facing into the wind and rain commanded, "Be still!" At once the wind and waves died down, and all was calm.

The disciples were amazed. "Who is this man?" they asked themselves. "Even the winds and waves obey him!"

Jesus Calms the Storm

If you have heard this story before, you may not be as impressed by Jesus's amazing power as if the story were new to you. Those who know the Bible risk thinking its familiar stories are ordinary. Many of us have "been here, heard that." How can you truly appreciate the wonder of Jesus's absolute control over nature?

We do not have the real Jesus lying in the bottom of our boat whenever we face danger. And because our world has been infected by sin, sometimes bad things happen. Have you asked Jesus a question like the disciples' frantic cry in Mark 4:38: "Teacher, don't you care if we drown?" Did Jesus answer? How and when?

Thank you, Creator God, for assuring me of your power and control over all things. Remind me that you always want the best for me, even when you allow bad things to happen. **Amen.**

Reflection Questions

1. Think of a time when God responded directly to your cry for help. How did that make you feel?

2. Now remember when God did not seem to be listening. He does not always explain his choices, but we know that "in all things God works for the good of those who love him" (Romans 8:28). How does that make you feel?

Action Points

1. Write out those words from Romans 8:28, or print them from the internet with a fancy font and add illustrations or photos. Give a copy to someone who needs it.

2. Make a list of your personal "top-ten Bible miracles." Even if they are familiar, stop to think about how amazing each one is. Be sure to thank God for them.

WALKING ON WATER
Matthew 14; Mark 6; John 6

Late one night, the disciples were back out on the lake, but Jesus had stayed ashore to pray. The waves tossed the boat violently. At dawn, the disciples saw a figure walking towards them on the water! They thought it was a ghost and were scared until they heard the calm voice of Jesus: "It is I. Do not be afraid."

Simon Peter was the first to speak. "Lord," he said, "if it is you, command me to walk across the water to you," and Jesus did so.

Peter put one foot gingerly in the water. Then he lowered the other and bravely stood up, letting go of the boat. He did not sink! But when he looked around at the waves, his courage failed him. As he began to sink, he cried, "Lord, save me!"

Jesus reached out and took his hand. "Oh, Peter," he said sadly, "where is your faith? Why did you doubt?" Then together they walked back to the boat. The wind died down, and the water became calm. The disciples bowed low. "Truly you are the Son of God," they said humbly.

Walking on Water

Have you ever talked to someone who does not believe in miracles? Maybe they think believing in such things is nonsense. The Bible says the disciples did not understand the miracle that took place just before this story (Jesus feeding more than 5,000 people with only five loaves and two fish) because "their hearts were hardened" (Mark 6:52). We need soft hearts to accept the Bible's miracle stories. Open and trusting hearts are gifts from God!

We live in a world that demands scientific proof. What this world does not recognise is that the Creator of the universe holds the power—and has the right—to make exceptions to his own natural laws. He does not always explain why he chooses to perform miracles, but they definitely catch our attention!

Awesome Lord, thank you for creating the universe (including me). Thank you for preserving and protecting it, for reaching out to me when I'm in trouble, and for softening my heart so I can believe in you. **Amen.**

Reflection Questions

1. Do you believe miracles still happen today? Can you give examples? (You might want to ask a parent, teacher, or priest for help.)

2. Have you ever trusted God until—like Peter in the story—your imagination took over and worry started to drown out your faith? How did the story end for you?

Action Points

1. Draw or paint a picture showing Jesus walking on the water towards the disciples in their fishing boat. Add detail, including the disciples' fear, the darkness and crashing waves, a wild-eyed Peter beginning to sink, and Jesus's loving expression as he reaches out his hand to save Peter.

2. Make and decorate a bookmark for your Bible with these words from Matthew 14:27: "Take courage! It is I. Don't be afraid."

JESUS AND THE CHILDREN
Matthew 19; Mark 10; Luke 18

Jesus loved little children, for they were good and innocent. He was always surrounded by children, and sometimes his disciples tried to shoo them away. "Do not stop little children from coming to me," he told them sternly. "The kingdom of heaven belongs to them and all those like them."

Once when the disciples began arguing about which of them was the most important, Jesus beckoned to a little child and put his arm around him. He turned to his disciples, saying, "Whoever welcomes this child in my name welcomes me, and whoever welcomes me welcomes the one who sent me. For it is the one who is least among you who is the greatest. To enter heaven, you must be like a little child!"

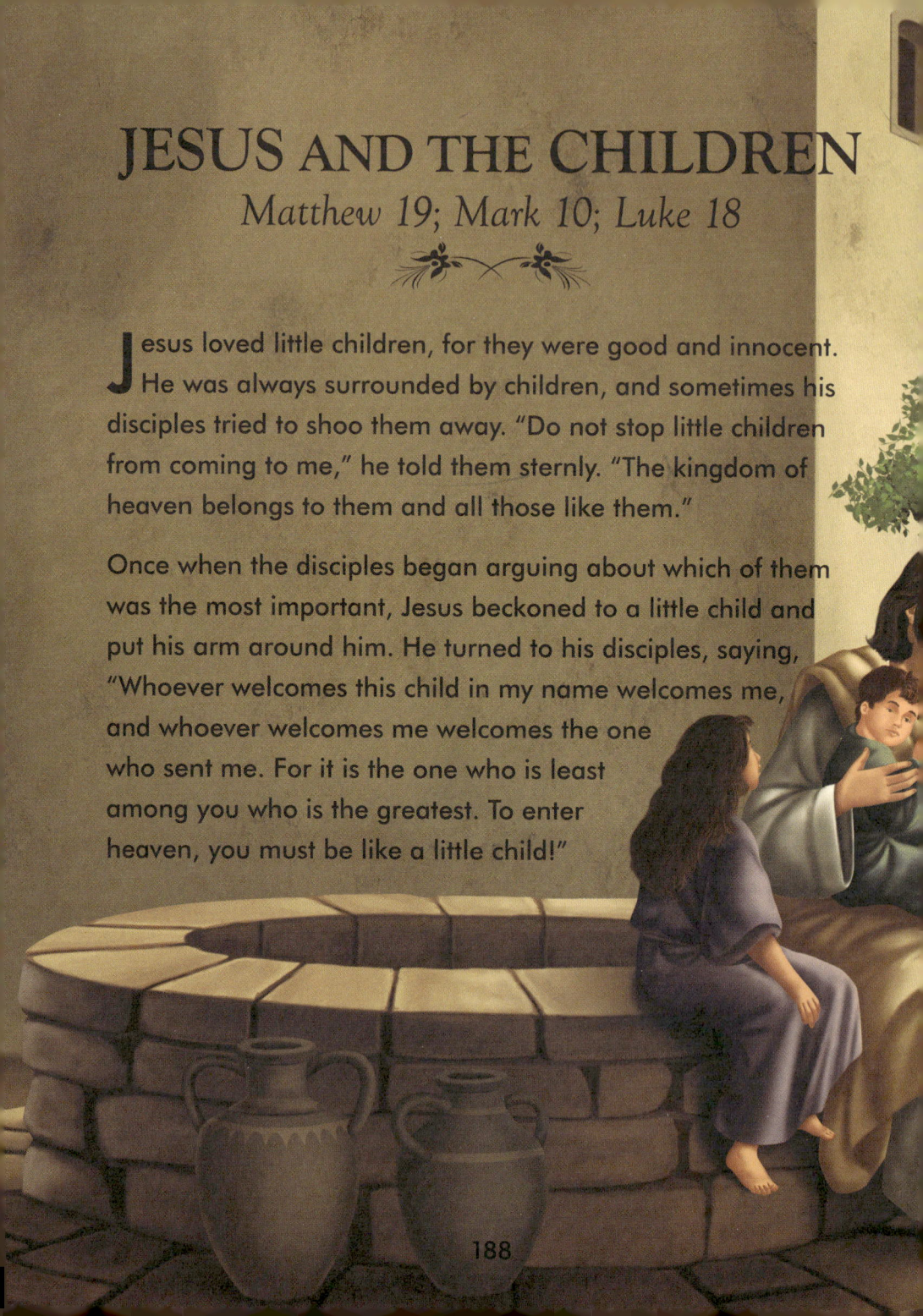

Jesus and the Children

What is it about little kids that makes them so trusting and eager to accept God's love? Maybe their inability to control their own lives makes them content to rest in Jesus's love and power. As we grow older, our pride can get the better of us, and we may begin to see life as a gigantic competition. Sometimes we want to be the boss, but the universe already has a Boss!

Many grown-ups have a hard time bowing before their Creator and Saviour. They have a hard time admitting they can't climb to heaven on their own. They may want to help Jesus out by being good instead of admitting they need *his* goodness. That would be like denying his perfect sacrifice on the cross for their sin! They may want to rule their own personal kingdom instead of benefiting from little kid-dom!

> **Dear God,** please help me to be soft and mouldable, loving and trusting, humble and willing. Hold me back from needing to add my goodness to your sacrifice. **Amen.**

Reflection Questions

1. Try to remember your earliest days with Jesus. How did you feel about him then? How is that relationship changing as you are growing up?

2. If kind actions can't earn your salvation, what is the point of doing them?

Action Points

1. Volunteer to spend a Sunday morning helping with your church's preschool class. Ask the teacher in advance how you can contribute.

2. Write a poem or song based on this story and share it with your family.

THE GOOD SAMARITAN

Luke 10

Once someone asked Jesus what the Law meant when it said we must love our neighbours as much as ourselves. "But who is my neighbour?" he asked, and Jesus told him a story:

"A man was going from Jerusalem to Jericho when he was attacked by robbers, who beat him and took everything from him before leaving him by the roadside half dead. Soon a priest passed by. When he saw the man, he crossed to the other side of the road and hurried on his way. Then a Levite came along. He also hurried on his way without stopping.

"The next person to come along was a Samaritan, who belonged to a group not friendly to the Jews. Yet when this traveller saw the man lying bleeding by the roadside, his heart was filled with pity. He knelt beside him and carefully washed and bandaged his wounds before taking him on his donkey to an inn, where he gave the innkeeper money to look after the man until he was well."

Jesus looked at the man who had posed the question and asked who he thought had been a good neighbour to the injured man.

The man sheepishly replied, "The one who was kind to him."

Then Jesus told him, "Go then, and be like him."

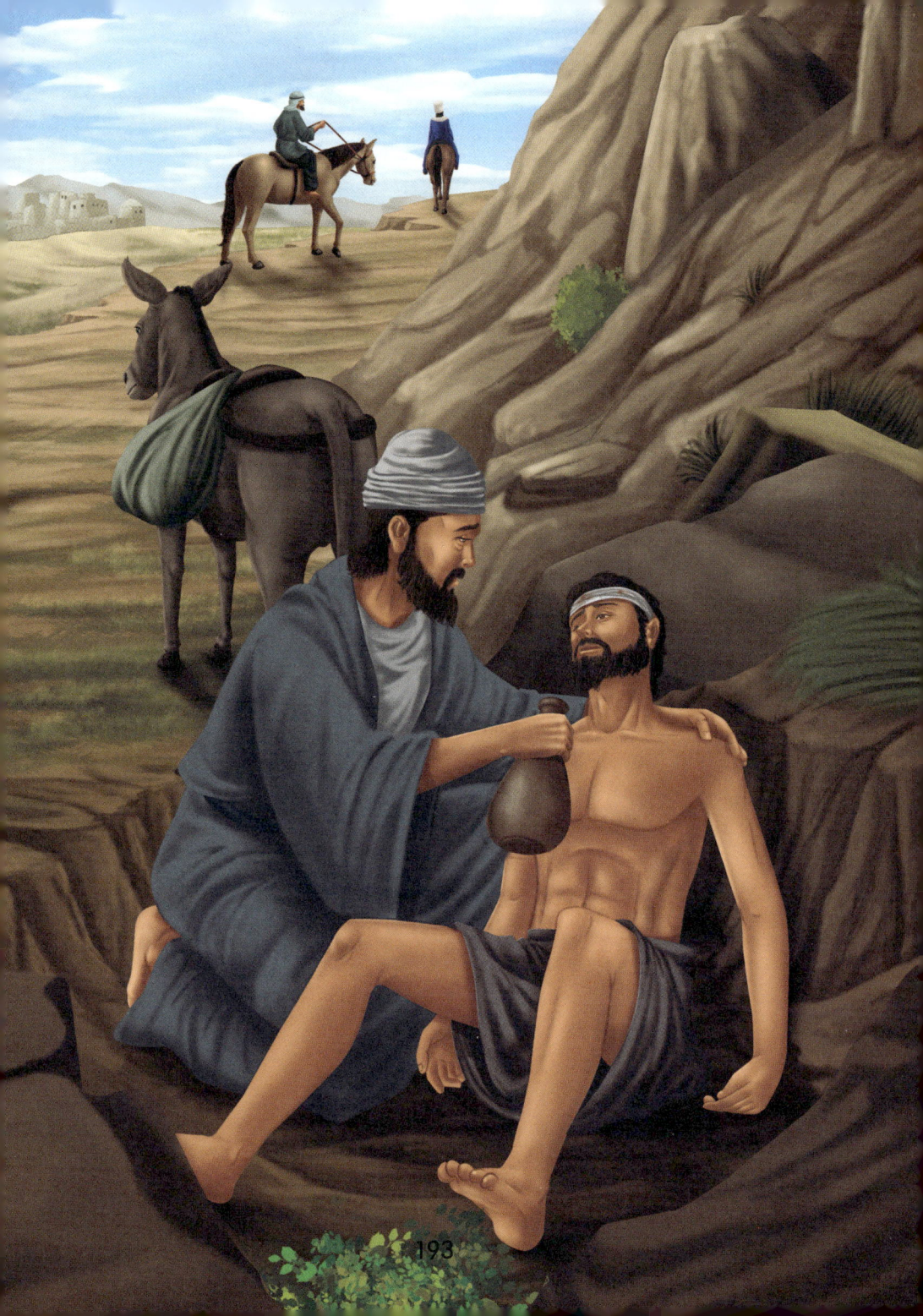

The Good Samaritan

The man who started this conversation was pretty sure of himself when it came to the complicated Jewish religious law. Page through Leviticus and Numbers in the Old Testament, reading some titles. Here are a few from the NIV: "Regulations About Defiling Skin Diseases," "Eating Blood Forbidden," "Unacceptable Sacrifices," and "Offerings for Unintentional Sins." The Jewish people had to learn these things with no internet or library books to remind them.

This man understood Jesus's message that loving God and our neighbours pretty much guarantees we will do the right thing. If we treat others fairly, we probably will not break a law. But there had to be a catch. Just *whom* did he have to treat fairly? Surely Jesus could not mean everybody. *Wrong*—that's exactly what Jesus meant!

Dear Jesus, help me follow your example of loving all people regardless of what I feel or think about them. **Amen.**

Reflection Questions

1. Do you think Jesus wants you to let people bully you? Or to ignore stranger danger? How can you love someone who is not good or safe for you?

2. Are all people (including terrorists) created in God's image and loved by him? Do Christians have the right to withhold mercy from those we see as his enemies?

Action Points

1. Be a good Samaritan to at least one person this week. Share your experience with your family at dinnertime.

2. Write these words of Jesus on a card and post it where you'll see it every day: "In everything, do to others what you would have them do to you, for this sums up the Law and the Prophets" (Matthew 7:12).

JESUS ENTERS JERUSALEM

Matthew 21; Mark 11; Luke 19; John 12

Jerusalem was packed. It was the week of the Passover festival, and everyone had gathered to celebrate. It was also time for Jesus to start the last stage of his earthly life.

Jesus entered Jerusalem riding a humble donkey. Some of his followers threw their cloaks or large palm leaves on the dusty ground before him, and he was met by an enormous crowd, for many had heard of the miracles he had performed. The religious leaders might have feared and hated Jesus, but many of the people truly saw him as their king, and they tried to give him a king's welcome.

His followers cried out, "Hosanna to the Son of David! Blessed is the king who comes in the name of the Lord!"

But Jesus was sad, for he knew that in a very short time these people cheering him would turn against him.

Jesus Enters Jerusalem

The Bible tells more of this story. After the unexpected "parade," the grown-ups stopped shouting their praise, but the kids kept on. They were prancing around outside the temple and yelling, "Hosanna!" There's something so genuine about the praise of kids—it makes friends happy, but it makes enemies angry. "Do you hear what these children are saying?" the teachers asked Jesus. Their angry tone implied, "Can you *believe* this?"

"Yes," Jesus answered. "Have you never read, 'From the lips of children and infants you, Lord, have called forth your praise'?" (Matthew 21:16). Jesus was talking about Psalm 8:2: "Through the praise of children and infants you have established a stronghold against your enemies, to silence the foe and the avenger." How did the tribute from these enthusiastic kids silence Jesus's enemies? How did God use their happy song to shame his enemies and guarantee his praise?

Dear Lord, please accept my praise and use it for your glory. **Amen.**

Reflection Questions

1. These kids were old enough to wander the streets unsupervised, but they were still young. How does it make you feel to know that God values your worship that much?

2. Kids often let their true feelings show, but sometimes grown-ups put on a show to get something they want. Why did the children's praise make them angry?

Action Points

1. Write a psalm of praise, including words from Matthew 21:9-10: "Hosanna to the Son of David! Blessed is he who comes in the name of the Lord! Hosanna in the highest heaven!" Either make it into a poster or plan music and dance steps to go with it.

2. Get help acting out the story of Jesus's entry into Jerusalem. Perform the play for your family and friends.

BETRAYAL

Matthew 26; Mark 14; Luke 22

Jesus knew that the Pharisees and those who hated and feared him were waiting for any opportunity to arrest him. He spent the days in Jerusalem in the temple, but each night he returned to Bethany to sleep. Yet even among his dearest friends there was one who would be his enemy.

Judas Iscariot, the disciple in charge of the money, was dishonest. He kept some for himself instead of giving it to those who

needed it. His greed made him do a very bad thing. Judas went to the chief priests in secret and asked them how much they would give him if he delivered Jesus into their hands.

The priests couldn't believe their ears! They knew that Judas was one of Jesus's closest, most trusted friends. They offered him 30 pieces of silver...and Judas accepted! From then on, Judas was simply waiting for the opportunity to hand Jesus over.

Betrayal

How sad… Judas identified Jesus for the soldiers by walking up and kissing him on his cheek! In those days it was not unusual for men to greet each other that way. This custom is still followed in parts of our world. The kiss was supposed to show respect and friendliness—not betrayal.

Is it possible for *you* to betray Jesus with a kiss? You cannot actually kiss him. But what about giving him what is sometimes called "lip service" (saying one thing while doing or thinking something quite different)? Like singing or joining in a unison prayer or reading at church or claiming to love Jesus—all without engaging your heart?

Lord and Savior, how sad Judas's kiss of betrayal must have made you! Help me to "kiss" you as a signal of my respect and love! **Amen.**

Reflection Questions

1. What less-than-loving thoughts or feelings get in your way while you are trying to honour Jesus with your words or behaviour?

2. Think back to a time when your words or actions betrayed your Lord. Your friends may know you as a Christian, but when did a temper tantrum or other behaviour send a different message?

Action Points

1. As you worship this week, do your best to line up your thoughts and feelings with your words and actions. This will be harder than it sounds! Think and pray about where you got off track.

2. Kiss your mum or dad and mean it! Make your kiss a signal of love.

A COCK CROWS

Matthew 26; Mark 14; Luke 22; John 18

The Jewish leaders hated Jesus and sent soldiers to arrest him. They took Jesus to the courtyard of the high priest to be questioned. Simon Peter followed them and waited outside, warming himself with some guards by a fire. A servant girl walked by and saw Peter standing there. "Weren't you with Jesus of Nazareth?" she asked him. "I'm sure I saw you with him."

"No, you've got the wrong man!" Peter hissed quietly, hoping no one else had heard, for he feared what would happen if they believed he was one of Jesus's disciples.

The girl shrugged and walked away, but on her way back, she said to one of the guards, "Don't you think he looks like one of Jesus's followers?"

"I told you, I don't have anything to do with him!" panicked Peter.

Now the other guards were looking at him. "You must be one of them," said a guard. "I can tell from your accent you're from Galilee."

"I swear I've never even met him!" cried Peter, his heart racing. At that very moment, a cock crowed, and Peter broke down and wept in dismay.

A Cock Crows

Claiming you are not going to sin does not sound so bad, does it? At least you are not intentionally lying. Pretending you haven't already blown it when you actually have—that's worse, isn't it?

Peter was very sure of himself when denying he would sin: "Even if all fall away on account of you, I never will," and "Even if I have to die with you, I will never disown you" (Matthew 26:33,35). He meant well, but pride got in his way. Then fear took over, and Peter cracked under the pressure—three times.

What tripped up Peter? Was it pride or fear or a combination of things? Emotions are not sinful; they are wonderful gifts from God. But sin usually starts with emotion. How you handle your emotions often determines the kind of life you will live.

Dear God, thank you for the gift of my emotions. Help me to honour you in the way I handle them. **Amen.**

Reflection Questions

1. Two of Peter's positive emotions were love and determination. Was his original intention to stand by Jesus at all costs a good thing or a bad thing?

2. Which emotions tend to get you into trouble? Which ones are strengths for you?

Action Points

1. Make an emotions chart. Along the left side list five emotions. Fold the paper in half the long way, labelling the two columns positive and negative. Write down times when you handled each emotion well and not so well.

2. Think back on your day so far. What emotions have motivated your actions?

THE DEATH OF JESUS
Matthew 27; Mark 15; Luke 23; John 19

The Jewish leaders convinced the Roman governor to have Jesus killed. Soldiers beat him and mocked him and nailed his hands and feet to a cross. But Jesus said, "Father, forgive them. They don't know what they are doing." Later, he cried out, "It is finished!" and with these words, he gave up his spirit.

At that moment, the earth shook, and the curtain in the holy temple was torn from top to bottom. When the Roman soldiers felt the ground move beneath their feet and saw how Jesus passed away, they were deeply shaken. "Surely he was the Son of God!" whispered one in amazement.

209

The Death of Jesus

Some weird and wonderful things happened the day Jesus died. Imagine how sad the angels must have been, remembering their joyful wonder on the night of his birth. Imagine standing at the foot of the cross, gazing up at Jesus with awe and terror. Then an eclipse blackened the afternoon sky, erasing the picture from your sight. Imagine trying to regain your balance as an earthquake shivered the ground and split the rocks around you. Imagine your horror as tombs split open and dead people came out. Imagine trembling at the rumour that the temple curtain had torn itself in two. Then you heard the Roman centurion gasp in whispered awe, "Surely this man was the Son of God!" (Mark 15:39).

That soldier recognised what so many could not—or would not! What about you? How would you have responded if you had been there? How would you have been changed?

No words could ever be enough, **Lord Jesus,** to thank you for your incredible gift on that day you died for me. Accept my love and praise, as poor as they are. **Amen.**

Reflection Questions

1. The Jews were eagerly waiting for their promised Messiah, or Saviour. So why did so many of them, including their religious leaders, reject Jesus? In what ways was he not what they expected?

2. We call that day of Jesus's death "Good Friday." But why— what was good about it?

Action Points

1. Write a poem-prayer thanking Jesus for his gift of eternal life.

2. How might your life have been different if Jesus had not taken your punishment to free you from sin and death? List as many points as you can.

THE EMPTY TOMB

Matthew 28; Mark 16; Luke 24; John 20

Early on the first day of the week, before the sun had fully risen, Mary Magdalene and some other women went to anoint Jesus's body. As they came near the tomb, the earth shook, the guards were thrown to the ground, and the women saw that the stone had been rolled away from the entrance. And inside the tomb, shining brighter than the sun, was an angel!

The terrified women fell to their knees, but the angel said, "Why are you looking for the living among the dead. He is not here—he has risen! Don't you remember that he told you this would happen? Look and see, then go and tell his disciples that he will meet them in Galilee as he promised."

So the women hurried away to tell the disciples the news, afraid yet filled with joy.

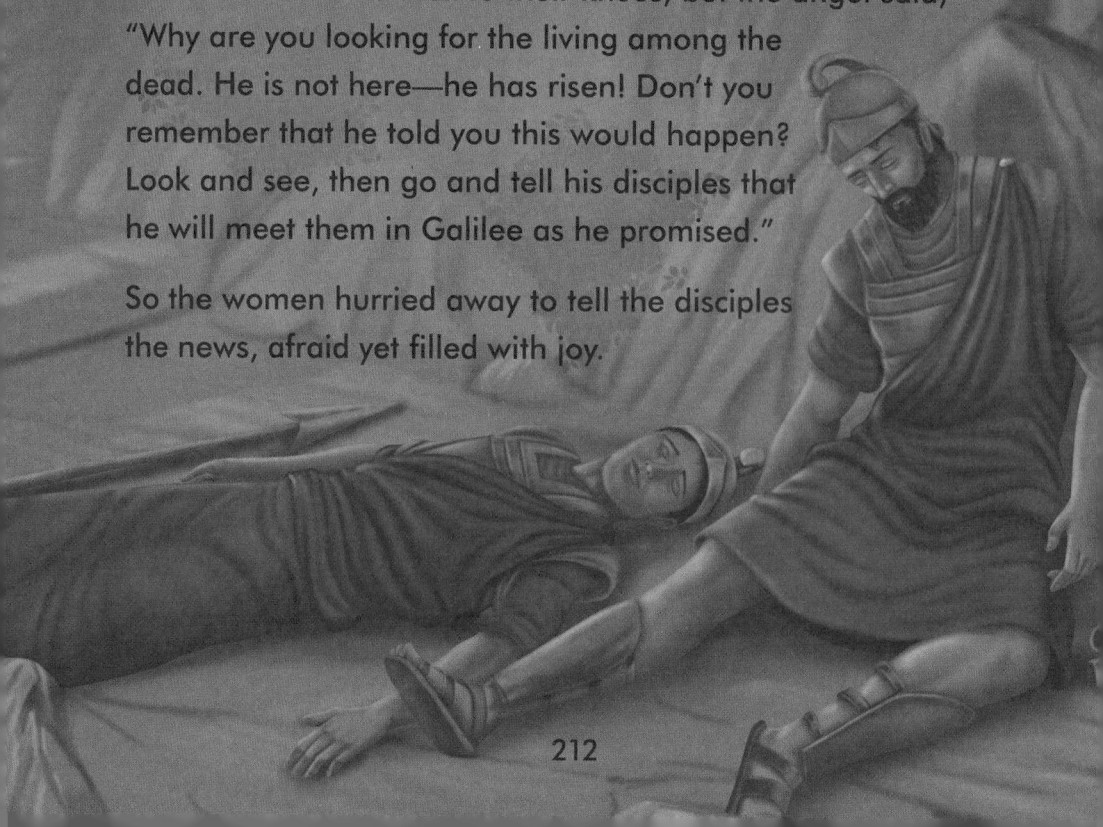

The Empty Tomb

Christmas is most people's favourite holiday, but only Christians appreciate its true meaning. Many see it as the central event in history, the point at which God appeared in the flesh as Immanuel (which means "God with us").

But Christmas would lose its meaning without Easter. Jesus's resurrection is the *real* centre of history. Jesus was born to die, but it was his rising from death that clinched his victory. The apostle Paul says, "If Christ has not been raised, our preaching is useless and so is your faith" (1 Corinthians 15:14).

Jesus's coming at Christmas took place in the darkness of night and sin. God pierced that darkness by an angel choir and an unusually bright star. But Easter dawns with the glory of sunrise—the full light of salvation!

> Remind me, **Jesus,** that your empty tomb makes life worthwhile. **Amen.**

Reflection Questions

1. Who would have won the victory for human souls if Jesus had stayed in the tomb? What would our world be like without the hope of salvation?

2. John 20:9 tells us that the disciples did not understand from Scripture that Jesus had to rise from the dead. Does this surprise you? After everything Jesus had said and done, why do you think they did not understand?

Action Points

1. Tell a friend the true meaning of Easter. It is not about spring, bunnies, chicks, or coloured eggs, though it has everything to do with new life. Because Jesus's tomb is no longer occupied, your grave can one day be empty too.

2. Write a song or poem celebrating what Jesus's resurrection means to you.

ALIVE!

Matthew 28; Mark 16; John 20

Mary Magdalene stood outside the tomb. Peter and one of the other disciples had come, had seen the strips of linen, and had left in wonder and confusion. Now she was alone. She missed Jesus so much.

Just then she heard steps behind her, and a man asked, "Woman, why are you crying? Who are you looking for?"

Thinking this must be the gardener, she begged, "Sir, if you have moved him, please tell me where he is, and I will get him."

The man only spoke her name, "Mary," but instantly she spun around. She recognised that clear, gentle voice!

"Teacher!" she gasped and reached out towards Jesus.

Jesus said, "Do not hold on to me, for I have not yet ascended to my Father. Go and tell the others!" So Mary rushed off with the amazing news that she had seen Jesus alive!

Alive!

An empty tomb was one thing—scary and confusing and hopeful and sad all at the same time. Encountering Jesus, alive and talking in that familiar voice, must have been quite another! Had the events of the past days been some terrible nightmare? Was an explanation even possible or necessary? Might it make the most sense to simply accept the impossible and respond in love and worship, as Mary did? To reach out trembling fingers that longed to touch?

Jesus's death had seemed so unbelievable and yet so final. So many had pinned their hopes on this much-loved Teacher and miracle worker, only to have their hopes replaced by confusion and despair. Jesus had predicted his death, it was true, but those who loved him had closed their ears to the unthinkable. What in the world was going on?

Accept the thanks of my overflowing heart, **dear Jesus.** I offer my love and my life to use in your service. **Amen.**

Reflection Questions

1. What in the world *was* going on that day Jesus showed he was alive again? How would the world be forever changed?

2. It is good and necessary to understand the importance of Jesus's resurrection for your salvation. But how do you *feel* about it? Share your emotions with Jesus.

Action Points

1. Share your feelings about the resurrected Jesus in other ways too. Share your excitement—not just your knowledge—with someone who needs to hear it.

2. Offer your service to Jesus in some specific way—not because you have to, but because you love him.

THE ASCENSION
Mark 16; Luke 24; Acts 1

After Jesus rose from the dead, he appeared many times to his disciples, proving that he was alive and teaching them about the kingdom of God. But after almost six weeks, the time had come for Jesus to leave the world.

Jesus turned to his disciples. "You must stay here in Jerusalem for now and wait for the gift that my Father has promised you, for soon you will be baptized with the Holy Spirit. Then you must spread my message not only in Jerusalem and Judea and Samaria, but in every country."

He held up his hands to bless them and then, before their eyes, he was taken up to heaven, and a cloud hid him from sight.

As they stood looking upwards in wonder, suddenly two men dressed in white stood beside them. "Why are you looking at the sky? Jesus has been taken from you into heaven, but he will come back again in the same way that he left!"

The Ascension

Isn't it great when someone you really like invites you to sit with them at lunch, hang out at their house after school, or maybe go somewhere fun together on the weekend? It makes you feel special to be included, doesn't it? You realise that person enjoys being with you. They like you!

Did you know that's how God feels about you? That's what the ascension is all about. When Jesus returned to his Father in heaven, he blazed a trail for us to follow. God wants us all to be with him! And for now, while our bodies are still on earth and we can't see God with our eyes, he has sent his Spirit to live in our hearts.

God has given you the best invitation ever!

Dear God, thank you so much for making a way for us to be with you. I accept your invitation! **Amen.**

Reflection Questions

1. Think of a time when someone invited you to do something really fun with them. Write down some words that describe how that made you feel.

2. God wants to be included in every part of your day. List some places you'll be this week or some things you'll do. Invite God to be with you in every one, and imagine him there with you.

Action Points

1. Find someone who looks like they could use an invitation, and ask them to do something fun with you. Do you know who you'll ask and what you'll do together?

2. Write this on a piece of paper and set it where you'll see it every day: "God is inviting me to be with him!"

There's So Much More to Explore in God's World!

If you like this devotional, there's more knowledge out there to discover. These three books will help you learn about the people, places, and words of the Bible in a fun and colourful way. Packed with awesome pictures and facts, The Complete Illustrated Children's Bible books are the perfect way to discover all the amazing things in God's Word.

Tell your parent about this page and have them look these books up for you. And keep reading your Bible. It's a great adventure!

The Complete Illustrated Children's Bible
The Complete Illustrated Children's Bible Atlas
The Complete Illustrated Children's Bible Dictionary

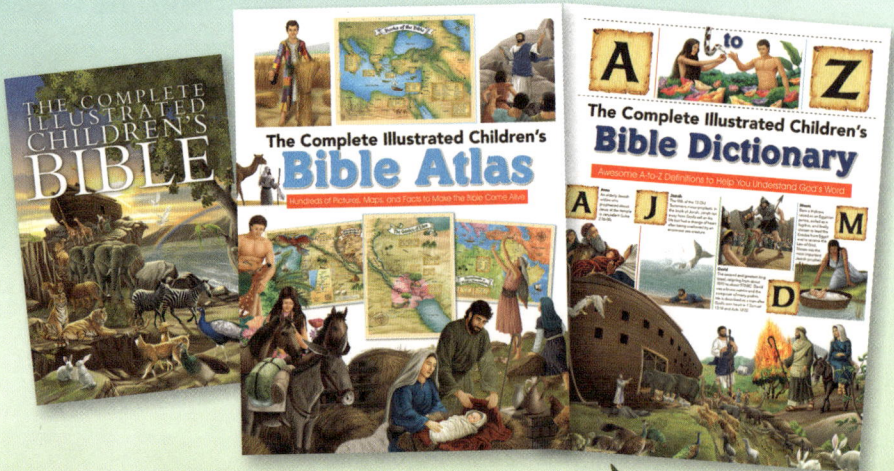